*The
Vancouver
Voyages
of the
Barque*

PAMIR

Profile of the barque *Pamir*.

The Vancouver Voyages of the Barque
PAMIR

RICHARD E. WELLS

1992

Sono Nis Press
VICTORIA, B.C., CANADA

Copyright © 1992 Richard E. Wells

Canadian Cataloguing in Publication Data

Wells, R. E. (Richard E.)
    The Vancouver voyages of the barque Pamir

ISBN 1-55039-029-5

    1. Pamir (Bark) – History. 2. Coastwise
shipping – British Columbia – History. 3.
Seafaring life – British Columbia – History.
I. Title.
VK27.B7W44 1992   387.2'24   C92-091370-9

This book was published with the assistance of the
Canada Council Block Grant Program.

Published by
SONO NIS PRESS
1745 Blanshard Street
Victoria, B.C., Canada V8W 2J8

Designed and printed in Canada by
MORRISS PRINTING COMPANY LTD.
Victoria, British Columbia

CONTENTS

Foreword / 7
Dedication / 9
Acknowledgements / 11

PART ONE   **THE VANCOUVER VOYAGES OF THE BARQUE PAMIR**

Introduction / 18
The First Vancouver Voyage / 23
The Second Vancouver Voyage / 43
The Third Vancouver Voyage / 63
After the Vancouver Voyages / 75
Men who sailed in the *Pamir* / 79

PART TWO   **THE TOWBOATS INVOLVED WITH THE BARQUE PAMIR**

Island Tug and Barge Limited / 91
The Halibut Steamers / 95
Island Commander / 105
Island Warrior / 111
Snohomish / 115
Robert Preston / 125

APPENDIX   Particulars of *Pamir* / 131
Voyages of the barque *Pamir* / 133

List of Illustrations

Profile of the barque *Pamir*, illustration by REW / Frontispiece
Pamir under full sail / 16
The First Vancouver Voyage: Inbound, illustration by REW / 22
                                  Outbound, illustration by REW / 35
The *Pamir* in tow of the *Island Commander* off Point Grey / 28
Scenes in Vancouver Harbour / 29, 30
The *Pamir* in Juan de Fuca Strait and off Cape Flattery / 30, 31
The First Voyage: Outbound – July 7-8, 1945 / 36, 37, 38, 39, 40
Map / 41
The Second Voyage: Inbound, illustration by REW / 42
                         Outbound, illustration by REW / 57
Figure 1, Tatoosh Island Weather Records November 1945, by REW / 44
Christmas 1945 – Menu / 50
Figure 2, Tatoosh Island Weather Records January 1946, by REW / 53
The Second Voyage: Outbound – January 5-6, 1946 / 58, 59, 60, 61
The Third Voyage: Inbound, illustration by REW / 62
                       Outbound, illustration by REW / 68
                       Outbound, illustration by REW / 69
                       Outbound, illustration by REW / 74
                       Outbound – August 3-5, 1946 / 70, 71, 72, 73
Magazine advertisement, Island Tug and Barge Ltd. / 90
Halibut Steamer in Gulf of Alaska / 94
The Halibut Steamers:
    Andrew Kelly – General Arrangement Plan, illustration by REW / 100
               – as commissioned / 101
               – as fishing trawler on Pacific coast / 101, 102
    George E. Foster – General Arrangement Plan, illustration by REW / 100
               – as fishing trawler on Pacific coast / 103
Island Commander – General Arrangement Plan; 1941 conversion,
          illustration by REW / 104
Island Commander / 108, 109, 110
Island Warrior / 113, 114
Snohomish – General Arrangement Plan 1908, illustration by REW / 119
         – General Arrangement Plan 1915, illustration by REW / 120
Snohomish / 121, 122, 123, 124
Robert Preston, Prestige II, Prestige / 128, 129, 130
Inside cover photos: Norman M. MacNeil

FOREWORD

Work shapes a man's life, possibly never more so than when that work is done on board a ship. This aphorism is probably not quite so true in today's seafaring life when the requisite work is conducted largely through the means of technological aids – push a button here, or flick a switch there, or pull a lever somewhere – and a mechanically devised response is almost instantly forthcoming. The seafarers of the recent past, however, had to depend on their hands, eyes and muscles, and on a personal perception on a one-to-one basis so as to sustain their ships and themselves at sea. This is a record from that era of seafaring; it is the memory of a ship (and the memoir of a sailor) and how she affected the lives of so many that came in contact with her – including that of the author.

The *Pamir* is notable in that she survived longer than almost all other vessels of her era, and in surviving, created a life and legend that has lived on after her departure.

This is not the complete history – that has been undertaken elsewhere in an exemplary record. Rather, this is a detailed look at the life of a working sailing ship, largely within British Columbia waters, presented in a manner that is most uncommon. The conjunction of the records of a sailing ship and of the powered vessels with which she was inevitably associated provide a unique approach to the documenting of maritime history, and the career descriptions of these associated powered ships complements the overall presentation.

Dick Wells speaks from personal experience – and from love of the seafaring life. He describes a way of life that has very largely vanished, and which is not to be characterized by "good riddance," but rather to be regarded with a feeling of deep loss. We have here, though, a small segment of that way of life as it took place in our coastal waters not too many years ago. For this we are profoundly grateful.

Leonard G. McCann, *Curator*
Vancouver Maritime Museum, September, 1991

DEDICATION

Behind every picture there is a story. The photographs reproduced in this book adequately depict the subjects: the sailing ship and the tugs; but beyond this, they were the result of one man's realization of the importance of recording for the future this maritime event. That man was Lt. Nicolas Beketov, RCN, who, in the mid-1940s was with the Intelligence Branch of the navy. He informed his friend, Gordon Moodie, that a sight to behold was soon to arrive at Vancouver and that it would be worthwhile for him to obtain a few pictures of it.

Both these men had met during the first years of the war when they were serving with the Air Force Marine Division. Flt. Sergeant Moodie was still with that branch of the Air Force. Beketov, formerly of the Russian Imperial Navy, was a lover of the sea and sailing ships, and knew that the *Pamir*'s visit to Vancouver was one that most probably would never occur again – and he was right.

And so, amateur photographer Gordon Moodie began taking the series of photographs with his old Leica 35mm camera that have become so well known and associated with the *Pamir* and that ship's visits to Vancouver. From the first views obtained during that late evening on 11 June 1945 from the cliffs at Point Grey, to the last scenes when the ship was photographed outbound under sail from the tug on which he had secured passage, Moodie obtained the many photographs which have continued to impress those who have admired and written about the ship. His attention to detail, enthusiasm, and composition of his scenes earned him much respect, and he and his family became great friends of the crew of the *Pamir* at the time.

The *Pamir* returned on yet another voyage to Vancouver, but this time without the restraints of wartime security. It was then that a second amateur photographer became involved with the ship. Norman M. MacNeil, with his speedgraphic camera, seasick and soaked, somehow managed to obtain the beautiful series of photographs on the outward tow from the tug *Snohomish*, photographs that have been acclaimed worldwide as the dramatic record of a large sailing ship underway in heavy weather. He too became a great friend of the *Pamir*'s crew.

When Moodie was on the tug during that first outbound voyage, MacNeil was up on Lions Gate Bridge photographing the tow as it passed out of Vancouver Harbour, and when MacNeil was on the tug during the second outbound voyage, Moodie was down at the North Vancouver waterfront recording the departure. He then sped out to Point Grey to catch the tow passing by that vantage point.

The *Pamir* came back once more, and this time Norman MacNeil was on hand in a small boat to record the departure from Union Bay, Vancouver Island. He then boarded the tug to obtain final departure photographs off Cape Flattery.

It is appropriate, therefore, to dedicate this book to the memory of these three men: Beketov, Moodie and MacNeil, without whose efforts and keen interest, the photographic documentation of this maritime event would not have occurred.

ACKNOWLEDGEMENTS

Much has been written about this famous sailing ship and her tragic loss in the Atlantic in 1957. Through the fates of war, she appeared here on the Pacific northwest coast during the 1940s – a last representative of the great age of commercial sail.

During that period, I worked on board the tow boats of Island Tug and Barge Limited of Victoria, British Columbia first as a "bargee" (the young fellow who steered the sailing ship hulls-cum-barges behind the tug) and then as deckhand, and was fortunate to have been on the last tow of the *Pamir* when aboard the tug *Island Warrior*.

Many years ago, during a visit to New Zealand, I met many of the *Pamir* crew members from those Vancouver voyages and learned details about these voyages from the men's own recollections. Records of communication and weather were obtained, and information was gathered from official government sources about the ship's operation while under the New Zealand flag. With help from these many sources, I wrote of the details and highlights of those Vancouver voyages in a two-part article that appeared in the Victoria *Daily Colonist* newspaper in February 1975. That account contained many interesting facts and correlations about the voyages that had not been reported before.

The account in this book is an extension and enlargement of the information in that article with special emphasis given to the tows (inbound and outbound) of the three voyages, and featuring photographs taken from and showing the Canadian tugs that were involved at the time. In this respect, Part II herein, gives the history of the tugs involved and the principal towing companies, and as well, remarks about the well-known skippers and mates who served on the tugs. The three appearances of this great ship on our coast received much publicity and, of course, the sight of such a ship under sail off Cape Flattery was captured on film and reproduced in several publications. Few photographs taken from the tugs showing the different scenes while under tow were published. Yet many were taken during these phases of the voyages, and it is due to the photographers, B. G. (Gordon) Moodie and Norman M. MacNeil, that the scenes of the outbound tows were recorded while they were passengers on board the tugs that performed the tows. These men also took photos of the *Pamir* at other times during the ship's visits.

I am indebted to Mrs. Margret Moodie of Vancouver, who has kindly allowed me to reproduce many of her late husband's beautiful photos, and to Mrs. Joan (MacNeil) Gutensohn of Maple Bay, Vancouver Island, who similarly has contributed many of her late father's fine photographs – all to achieve my desire to record this great maritime event of local towing history. The record of the third voyage tow is taken from a roll of 120 film I shot at the time using an old Brownie box camera, and some of Mr. MacNeil's photos.

There were others who obtained photographs, notably Mr. Hugh Frith of the Vancouver Harbour Board, who also went out on the *Snohomish* that day in early January 1946, and one of his photos was later used on an Island Tug and Barge Company calendar. And, many years later, some of the *Pamir* crew members contributed photographs taken during the Vancouver visits.

The appearance of this great ship on our coast was a significant historical event, and I have attempted to capture those moments during the three inbound and outbound tows in the illustrations presented in this book.

The following ex-*Pamir* men helped to make this account possible, in particular Captain D. W. (Bill) Galloway who was the harbourmaster, Port of Wellington, New Zealand, and former first mate of the *Pamir*, who gave freely of his time during my visit to New Zealand and showed me literally suitcases of files, clippings, and photographs from a great period in his life; Captain G. Inkster, also a harbourmaster, Port of Nelson, New Zealand, a former able seaman on the *Pamir*; Mr. W. D. Brereton and Mr. L. Healy, both former radio officers on the *Pamir* and although not members of the crew on the Vancouver voyages; Mr. Murray Henderson; Captain Ken Wells; and Mr. Robert Howard.

In addition, the following institutions in New Zealand were of great help: National Archives, Wellington; Alexander Turnbull Library, Wellington; Union Steamship Company of New Zealand Limited; Ministry of Transport, Marine Division, Wellington; New Zealand Ship and Marine Society; New Zealand *Pamir* Association; and the Wellington Harbour Board Maritime Museum.

In Canada, the reports contained in our own newspapers both in Vancouver and Victoria have been of assistance in correlating the various events.

The National Archives of Canada, the Vancouver Maritime Museum, the Vancouver Public Library and Vancouver City Archives, and the Vancouver Port Corporation were also helpful in the acquisition of photographs and data.

Lt.-Commander Charles Medley (RCN, retired) formerly of Naval Intelligence (Special Branch) provided useful information about wartime security on the Pacific coast at the time of the *Pamir*'s first visit.

Captain H. D. Huycke, a noted U.S. marine historian, assisted with information about the *Pamir* visits.

The U.S. National Oceanic Atmospheric Administration provided the Tatoosh Island weather records.

The book, *Pamir – The Story of a Sailing Ship* (1949) by Sydney Waters contained useful information about the *Pamir*'s Pacific voyages and was of great assistance in compiling details about the Vancouver voyages.

Another book most worthy of mention is *Mit der Pamir um Cap Horn* (1974) by the late Captain Heinze Burmester, which features among a group of photos, a fine view of the third-voyage departure from Union Bay, Vancouver Island (one of Norman MacNeil's photos) – a moment of special significance to me, as I was standing on the deck of the tug at that very moment. Mr. Burmester kindly donated the print of this photo. He was well qualified to write about the *Pamir*, for he served as an Ordinary Seaman on the ship in 1929 on a return voyage to Chile – one of the last of the nitrate Cape Horn passages – just before the *Pamir* was sold into the Erikson Fleet.

The Pamir under the New Zealand Ensign (1978) by Jack Churchouse is *the* record of all the voyages of the ship while she was under the New Zealand flag, and it is pleasing to observe that that author included many of the Moodie and MacNeil photos in his book. I met Mr. Churchouse in the early 1970s during a visit to New Zealand, and he was most helpful to me at a time when he was "buried" in his own research for his book.

The following, including many ex-crew members of the actual tugs, their families, collectors, and others, have made contributions of photos or helped with information: Captains George Dance; Frank Culbard; W. D. (Bill) Dolmage; G. W. (Joe) Higgs; Ken Higgs; Martin Higgs; Stu Hills; George Hovel; E. D. (Drydie) Jones; Korra Larsen; Wayne Lusk; D. G. MacPherson; Joe Quilty; Rollie Robinson; Jim Talbott; Al Zueff – all towboat skippers. Captain W. Hagelund; Commander Victor Johnson (USCG, retired), who commenced his career with the U.S. Coast Guard as a seaman on the *Snohomish* in 1922; Captain Heinze Burmester; Shirley Harlock, who was radio operator on the *Snohomish* in her first years with Island Tug; L. Amboldt; J. B. Ardizzone; M. Armstrong; Doreen (MacFarlane) Beattie; F. Heward Bell; Guillermo Berger; Pat Cavin; Ken Drushka; D. Elworthy; F. Grimble; R. Harvey; John Henderson; Dave Hood; Steven Lang; Harry McDonald; Gordon MacFarlane; Jim Owens; Brian Roberts; J. Robertson; George N. Y. Simpson; H. Tattersall; Mrs. W. Watmough; Johnny Walker; Gordon Whiting.

Mr. Len McCann, Curator of the Vancouver Maritime Museum, has always been helpful to those researching and writing about local marine topics.

The following companies and institutions were also of assistance in compiling the data about the tugs: National Library of Canada; Prince Rupert Regional Archives; B.C. Archives and Records Service; B.C. Maritime Museum; Vancouver Maritime Museum; Canadian Merchant Service Guild; Seaspan International Limited, Vancouver; Rivtow Straits Limited, Vancouver; Allied Shipbuilders Limited, Vancouver; Progress Publishing Company Limited, Vancouver; National Maritime Museum, Greenwich, London, England; Cochrane Shipbuilders Limited, Selby, England; Grimsby *Evening Telegraph*; Humberside Libraries and Arts Unit, Central Library, Hull, England; National Archives and Records Administration, Washington, D.C.; U.S. Coast Guard, Public Affairs Branch, Washington, D.C.; Puget Sound Maritime Historical Society; Washington State Historical Society; Coast Guard Museum Northwest, Seattle; International Pacific Halibut Commission; U.S. National Park Service Library, San Francisco (formerly the San Francisco Maritime Museum); Historical Division, Argentine Navy; Trans-Ona S.A.M.C.I.F., Buenos Aires.

Books which provided useful information about the tugs were: *Against Wind and Weather*, Drushka (1981); *The Pacific Halibut*, Bell (1981); *Fishing*, J. E. and A. D.

Forester (1975); *Ocean Highway*, Island Tug and Barge Limited; *Marine History of the Pacific Northwest*, McCurdy.

Abbreviations used on photo captions to denote photographer, where known, or source: ASL, Alaska State Library; AS, Allied Shipyards; BCARS, British Columbia Archives and Records Service; BCR, Brian C. Roberts; BD, Bill Dolmage; BGM, B. G. (Gordon) Moodie; CGMNW, Coast Guard Museum Northwest; FC, Frank Culbard; CDHS, Cumberland and District Historical Society; GET, Grimsby *Evening Telegraph*; GI, Gilbert Inkster; GMac, Gordon MacFarlane; GNYS, George N. Y. Simpson; HF, Hugh Frith; HMcD, Harry McDonald; KH, Ken Higgs; MMBC, Maritime Museum of B.C.; NAC, National Archives Canada; NMM, Norman M. MacNeil; PMRV, Princess Mary Restaurant vessel; PRRA, Prince Rupert Regional Archives; PSMHS, Puget Sound Maritime Historical Society; RCAF, Royal Canadian Air Force; REW, Richard E. Wells; SH, Stu Hills; VMM, Vancouver Maritime Museum; VPL, Vancouver Public Library; WSHS, Washington State Historical Society.

It is hoped that this account, together with the many fine photographs, will preserve forever those moments when the great age of sail made a last showing on our coast. I remember well not only the *Pamir* but also the tugs that towed her, and it has been a pleasure to chronicle their histories and assemble the photos from the many sources to illustrate their appearance over their working careers. It is hoped that those associated with the B.C. towing industry, past and present, and the general reader, will derive as much pleasure out of reading this book as I have had in assembling all the information.

The account is, indeed, a recollection of a significant event in British Columbia maritime history.

REW

Pamir under full sail.

PART ONE

THE VANCOUVER VOYAGES OF THE BARQUE *PAMIR*

Introduction

Many people on the west coast, particularly residents of Vancouver, will remember the barque *Pamir* when she made her three voyages here during the 1940s. There was much publicity about the ship's appearance and literally hundreds of photographs were taken of her. Her appearance on this coast was a vision out of the past and stirred the hearts of many, particularly those with past experience at sea and in sail. The sight of the *Pamir* was indeed one that was never to be seen again, and in this regard west-coast residents were fortunate to be able to have a glimpse of such an example of a bygone era. The *Pamir* was one of the few sailing ships that survived in ocean trade into the first few decades of the twentieth century, and she was an example of the ultimate development of the sailing ship: the large modern steel carriers with all their refinements. She was one of a fleet of German ships built especially for the nitrate trade from South America via Cape Horn to Europe. She had tremendous strength. Her loss in 1957, while serving as a cargo-carrying training ship, was viewed with alarm and sadness throughout the maritime world.

That the *Pamir* should appear in Vancouver can be attributed to the fate of war. At the time, in the early 1940s, this well-known ex-German ship was based in Finland and was one of a fleet that had been acquired by the Finnish ship owner, Gustav Erikson, whose ships were put into the grain trade from Australia in the 1930s. His was a last attempt to keep the sailing ship alive but, one by one, the ships were forced out of the trade by the economics of the time and their inability to compete with the modern steamship. Those ships that were kept in operation were directed anywhere a cargo could be loaded. As such, the *Pamir* found her way into the guano trade and had made a couple of voyages to New Zealand from the Seychelles. In August 1941, when berthed at Wellington to discharge guano, the *Pamir* was seized by the New Zealand government as a prize of war. Finland's hostility to Russia, then a member of the Allied cause, was justification for the seizure. When the *Pamir* appeared in Vancouver, she was being operated by the Union Steamship Company of New Zealand for the government of that country.

After an extensive refit, the big four-master was put into service in Pacific trade to the American west coast. Her re-commissioning to this service came at a time when tonnage was in short supply and the New Zealand government had decided that with prevailing freight rates there was a good possibility of the ship making profitable voyages. And so, after a period of eight months, the *Pamir* set sail on her first of eight voyages across the Pacific to the North American west coast with a crew made up predominantly of New Zealanders. Several of her former Finnish crew were retained, including one of the mates, the carpenter and sailmaker. The fact that the Union Steamship Company had men with experience in sail in its ranks was one of the deciding factors for putting the ship into trade. Except for the master and mates, and those retained from the former Finnish crew, the *Pamir* went to sea with an inexperienced crew, and responsibility thus lay heavily on the officers for the success of the voyage and the shaping up of a new crew.

When the news reached the New Zealand public that the *Pamir* would be put into service, there were applications from all parts of the country from boys and parents on behalf of their sons – all hoping for this great opportunity to go to sea in a real windjammer. And so, after careful selection, the ship put to sea from Wellington on her maiden voyage flying the New Zealand flag with 41 men aboard, compared to the 29 men she had under the Finnish flag. Included in the crew were 14 deck boys, 4 ordinary seamen, 12 able seamen, plus the master, mates, bosun, carpenter, sailmaker, cooks, stewards and radio officers. With a similar number of men, the ship made five voyages to San Francisco carrying wool and/or tallow (rendered animal fat) and miscellaneous general cargo back to New Zealand. The ship then made three voyages to the Canadian west coast – to Vancouver, British Columbia.

The recounting of this part of the *Pamir*'s history brings to light the way of life under sail. Many countries today believe in the value of training men under sail, even though this mode of maritime transport has long been succeeded by the modern propeller-driven ship. But, as pointed out by many master mariners, the essential asset is man, even in this atomic age. There is need for true seamen to man new ships and basic seamanship should not be forgotten even in the modern, highly technological navies. And to become a good seaman, the sailing ship is yet the best school. The trainee in sail learns that his work can be a test of courage, nerve, endurance and ability to react quickly and with good judgement in an emergency. This is the philosophy behind the sail training programmes undertaken by some countries today.

In this account about the *Pamir*, the reader will recognize certain situations where the ability of men trained in sail is demonstrated. The New Zealanders involved were fortunate to have the chance at such seafaring experience, and the result of this period in their young lives can be seen in the success most of them attained in not only the marine field but in other endeavours.

A quote from a master mariner will serve to adequately support the value of life and training under sail better than any layman's words:

> It was a life that taught self-reliance, for often enough a boy had to do his work alone with no one to advise or assist him. It taught power of decision, developed presence of mind and tested a man in endurance of both mental and physical strain – he emerged with a pretty fair idea of his own capability. A man who is sure of himself is most likely to do the right thing in his journey through life. In modern days, few young men know what they can take in life because they are seldom tested and they are generally the greatest losers by this. It is important that a man know himself before all things else.

This account about the *Pamir* goes a step further than just the precise details of the Vancouver voyages. Although details of subsequent voyages under New Zealand operation are mentioned and very brief information is included to round out the ship's history until her tragic loss, the intent has been to bring forth much of the "behind the scenes" information involving the ship's continued operation under the New Zealand flag. At the time, the economics of the *Pamir*'s continued operation were the subject of close scrutiny and review by the government amid growing suspicion that New Zealand would not be able to bear the financial drain of their prize. The ship's later voyages were showing substantial losses and in the face of this reality the government could not go on justifying its operation. The New Zealand public and those involved in the marine field supported retention of the ship at all costs. The high-level talks and decisions within the government about the fate of the *Pamir* finally resulted in the formal announcement being made that the ship would be returned to her former Finnish owners.

Such government discussion and decision was, at the time, confidential. The facts now revealed through perusal of the original files, courtesy of the New Zealand government, will be of interest to anyone who knew the *Pamir* and Canadians will be particularly interested because – of the several proposals that were received by the New Zealand government about the *Pamir*'s fate – one such scheme originated in western Canada involving the ship in a Commonwealth training programme. Other queries came in asking about the ship's possible sale. Another proposal involved her use under charter for a film. Such communications stirred the government departments involved into serious consideration about the ship's future. Voyage costs were continually escalating – new union agreements were contributory. Installation of auxiliary engines was considered to eliminate towage costs. Coastal trade was considered. The true economic situation about the *Pamir* at that time and the recounting of some of the internal moves by government, not widely known then or now, illustrates only too clearly the problem that earlier ship owners faced in trying to keep sailing ships paying their way.

Pamir meets *Island Commander* off Cape Flattery.

THE FIRST VANCOUVER VOYAGE

For the sixth voyage to North America, it was decided to send the ship to Vancouver, Canada, where a return cargo of wheat had been arranged. The possibilities of sending the ship into the Indian Ocean to re-enter the guano trade had been considered before she came back from her last San Francisco voyage, but wartime was considered too dangerous to send the vessel into that area.

There was consideration for her use as a training ship but the *Pamir* was not the property of New Zealand, being then employed by the government after the Prize Court had released the vessel to the Crown. These considerations continued and the government had to decide if and when to take title to the vessel before any such plan or other employment could be carried out.

It is interesting to note that the earnings of the *Pamir* had fallen off from the first three financially successful voyages when she earned £15,400, £23,800 and £29,400 respectively, which were the result of full-capacity loadings northbound and comparatively low stevedoring costs. But the fourth and fifth voyages to San Francisco resulted in losses of £1,700 and £500 respectively – the result of only part cargoes with higher stevedoring costs. These figures were subsequently revised to reflect the amounts originally spent to ready the vessel for her first voyage – over £20,000 – and take account of other accounting corrections. The figures thus became: First Voyage (unchanged), profit £15,400; Second Voyage, profit £15,700; Third Voyage, profit £14,600; Fourth Voyage (unchanged), loss £1,700; Fifth Voyage, loss £7,600.

And so, the diminished returns of the *Pamir*'s last San Francisco voyages were very much contributory to her re-employment in Pacific trade, but this time to Vancouver, British Columbia, where the discharge of an inward cargo of approximately 1,000 tons of tallow had been arranged through London and Canadian authorities. It was hoped that on this voyage, the *Pamir* would again show a profit.

The *Pamir* departed Wellington on 13 April 1945 after having been in port little more than a month after her last arrival from San Francisco. Favoured by strong westerlies, she made good time across the South Pacific for the first two weeks. The best day's run of the passage was on 25 April when she logged 290 miles, and during four days to noon of the 28th she covered 915 miles. En route, VE (Victory in Europe) Day was celebrated (9 May) and flags were flown, but the ship was still proceeding under wartime regulations as hostilities with Japan were still not over. As such, strict radio silence was being maintained and no lights were shown. Ship's boats were swung out over the side in case of any encounter with an enemy submarine. The *Pamir* was, of course, a sitting duck, and had had a previous encounter with a submarine on her last voyage northward to San Francisco when fortunately, no hostile action took place. The *Pamir* crossed the equator on 12 May and the ship's newspaper, *Pamir Press* noted that they had crossed the "Line" five times in the past twelve months – an excellent performance for a sailing ship.

At Vancouver, the Canadian Australasian Line had agreed to act as agents for the ship and the matter of towage had been looked into. In New Zealand on former voyages, towage had been a costly part of the ship's operation, because tug crews received a war-risk bonus and war-risk insurance was necessary for tugs. The Union Steamship Company of New Zealand had reduced these costs by using their own coastal steamers for towing the vessel to and from port.

On the Pacific coast, however, this was not deemed to be a problem because there were many tugs available at any time, and particularly there were several deep-sea tugs which were used for taking sailing ship hulls (hog-fuel barges) up and down the Juan de Fuca Strait and off Cape Flattery. Accordingly, Island Tug and Barge Limited of Victoria, B.C., entered into an agreement with the ship's agents: for a flat rate, they would pick up the *Pamir* off Cape Flattery, tow her to Vancouver, transfer her to a loading berth, and tow her back out to sea.

And thus, the well-known local tugs *Snohomish*, *Island Commander* and *Island Warrior* became involved with the *Pamir*. The first two of these were alternately on the run between Port Alberni, Vancouver Island, and Port Angeles and Port Townsend in Washington State with the hog-fuel barges.

On the ship's approach to the Juan de Fuca Strait, records noted westerly squalls as the *Pamir* stood in towards our coast on an east northeasterly course, and the crew were busy readying the ship to look smart for her first Canadian visit. After 59 days and 6 hours, the ship approached Swiftsure Bank (marked by a flashing buoy throughout the war years) on the evening of 10 June 1945 after having sailed 8,503 miles from Wellington at an average speed of nearly six knots.

Mr. W. D. Brereton, radio officer on this voyage, like many others who served aboard her, kept his own personal log and maintained a collection of photos and press clippings about the *Pamir*'s voyages, recorded the drama of that first landfall off the Juan de Fuca Strait:

> 10 June 1945. Land Ho. Fine on the port bow. Radioing for tug, customs, doctor, etc. Approached Juan de Fuca Strait about 11 a.m. Weather thickened and wind backed SE. We stood out to sea. Returned in afternoon with SW wind. Weather again thickened – obtained many radio bearings from Pachena Point and Tatoosh Island – excellent results. Asked Pachena for bearings every half hour – typical Canadian reply, "Sure, just call." Tug appeared at 9.30 p.m. Had difficulty getting towline aboard. Thick, but Swiftsure clearly visible. Radio messages sent VAK for forwarding to Comnowest seafron. Code used.

Mr. Brereton's log goes on to record the messages that he sent and received relative to their approach.

> To VAK
> 101400 Z: Hope arrive lightvessel 2340 GMT 10th require tug then – Master.
>
> To VAK
> 101718 Z: Cancel tug am standing to sea – Master.
>
> To VAK
> 101930 Z: Weather conditions entrance Strait. Wind now Southwest here – am standing in – Master.
>
> From Pachena Point VAD
> 102102 Z: Wind Southeast about 20 m.p.h. Visibility about 3 miles, light to moderate rain, barometer steady now.
>
> To VAK
> 102132 Z: Bearing 251° 35 miles from Swiftsure lightvessel. Course 081°. Speed 7-8 knots. Please dispatch tug to contact me there – Master.
>
> To VAK
> 110054 Z: Position 075° 20 miles. Course 081°. Speed 5 knots. Request tug proceed out from lightvessel to contact me – Master.

The Master, Captain A. R. Champion, was making his approach with caution to these waters known for "periods of thick weather and adverse currents" and the communications above demonstrate this caution. The frequent use of Pachena Point DF station in conjunction with the American station on Tatoosh Island, Washington, was at that time, before the use of radar and automatic shore beacons, a great aid to inbound shipping.

The *Pamir* carried a 250-watt transmitter which had a maximum range of about 300 miles. It is noted that the DF service was obtained by the use of code in accordance with the wartime regulations. Station VAK was Victoria Marine Radio, then Victoria Coast Guard Radio, although at that time this station was located at Gordon Head, a suburb of Victoria. Its location was then in the village of Sooke on the west coast of Vancouver Island, but has been recently closed with Vancouver Coast Guard Radio taking over all services. The notation 102132 Z refers to Greenwich time on the 10th and to reduce to the local time, which was then Pacific War Time, the same as Pacific Daylight Saving Time, 7 hours must be subtracted. "Comnowest seafron" refers to the Commander of the Northwest Sea Frontier, Headquarters, Thirteenth Naval District, U.S. Navy, which had overall jurisdiction of security at the time.

The tug involved was the *Island Commander*, an ex-North Sea trawler, and at the time one of the principal diesel tugs of Island Tug and Barge Ltd. of Victoria. She was painted in wartime grey. She came close in under the *Pamir*'s starboard side and the *Pamir*, with little way on together with her heavy top hamper of masts, spars and rigging, was rolling quite heavily in the swells, and the tug was given a good knock as the big steel hull rolled into it. With some difficulty, the towline was successfully passed and hove aboard. The time was 2130 (local time) and the tow into the Strait began.

Swiftsure Bank off the western entrance to the Juan de Fuca Strait and some 13 miles northwest of Tatoosh Island, had been marked for many years by a lightvessel. This strategic aid to navigation was under the control of the U.S. Coast Guard and during the war years had been replaced by a flashing buoy, the lightvessel itself being conscripted for wartime service. In 1946, after the war, the lightvessel was returned to this station but in 1961 this aid was removed and Swiftsure now remains unmarked.

Gilbert Inkster, then an AB (able-bodied seaman) on the *Pamir*, recalled that summer evening as he and his mates worked aloft for several hours getting all sail off and furled as they proceeded under tow. He remarked that being aloft when no sails were set made it seem a long way down to the deck – it was – the *Pamir*'s masts were 168 feet from deck to truck.

Customs, pilot and doctor came aboard from Victoria about 11:00 the following morning as the tow appeared off Victoria. Mr. Inkster recalled how beautiful it was towing up through the sounds (Gulf Islands), the late evening arrival under the Lions Gate Bridge and docking at the CPR pier by 10:30 that night. Other records mentioned a very talkative Canadian pilot aboard the ship, and on arrival at Vancouver the mounties (Royal Canadian Mounted Police) made a thorough search through the ship.

On this voyage 38 of her crew were New Zealanders. Her master was from Lyttelton. His brother, D. C. Champion, served as first mate. Andy S. Keyworth was second mate and F. M. Renner, third mate. The remainder of the New Zealand crew was made up as follows: 8 able seamen, 5 ordinary seamen, 10 deck boys, bosun and two mates, carpenter, motorman, radio officer and assistant, chief steward and assistant, and finally the chief cook and his assistant. Several others in the crew were of other nationalities.

After her arrival at Vancouver, the ship was the subject of great interest. In the days following and while her cargo was being unloaded, people lined the railings above the dock to get a glimpse of the ship; people visited the ship; and the press and others took photos, conducted interviews and wrote articles about the voyage and the crew. There was great publicity.

Crew members were entertained in private homes, struck up their own acquaintances, went up Grouse Mountain, Lynn Valley, the Capilano Suspension Bridge, and in general had some good times while in port. One specific recollection was when a party of Wrens (Royal Canadian Navy – women's force) came down to the ship and their commander thought that maybe it was unwise to go aboard. However, assurance was soon given that the bearded and bronzed types on board were harmless and just a bunch of down-to-earth friendly New Zealanders.

The first view of *Pamir* approaching Vancouver on the evening of 11 June, 1945.
Photo taken from Point Grey.

VMM

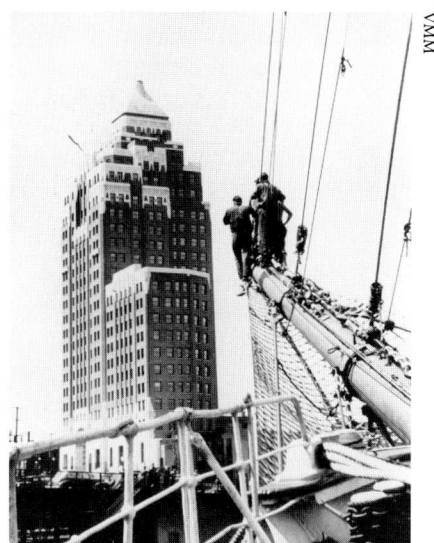

The *Pamir* alongside Pier B-C (CPR Pier) in front of the Marine Building.

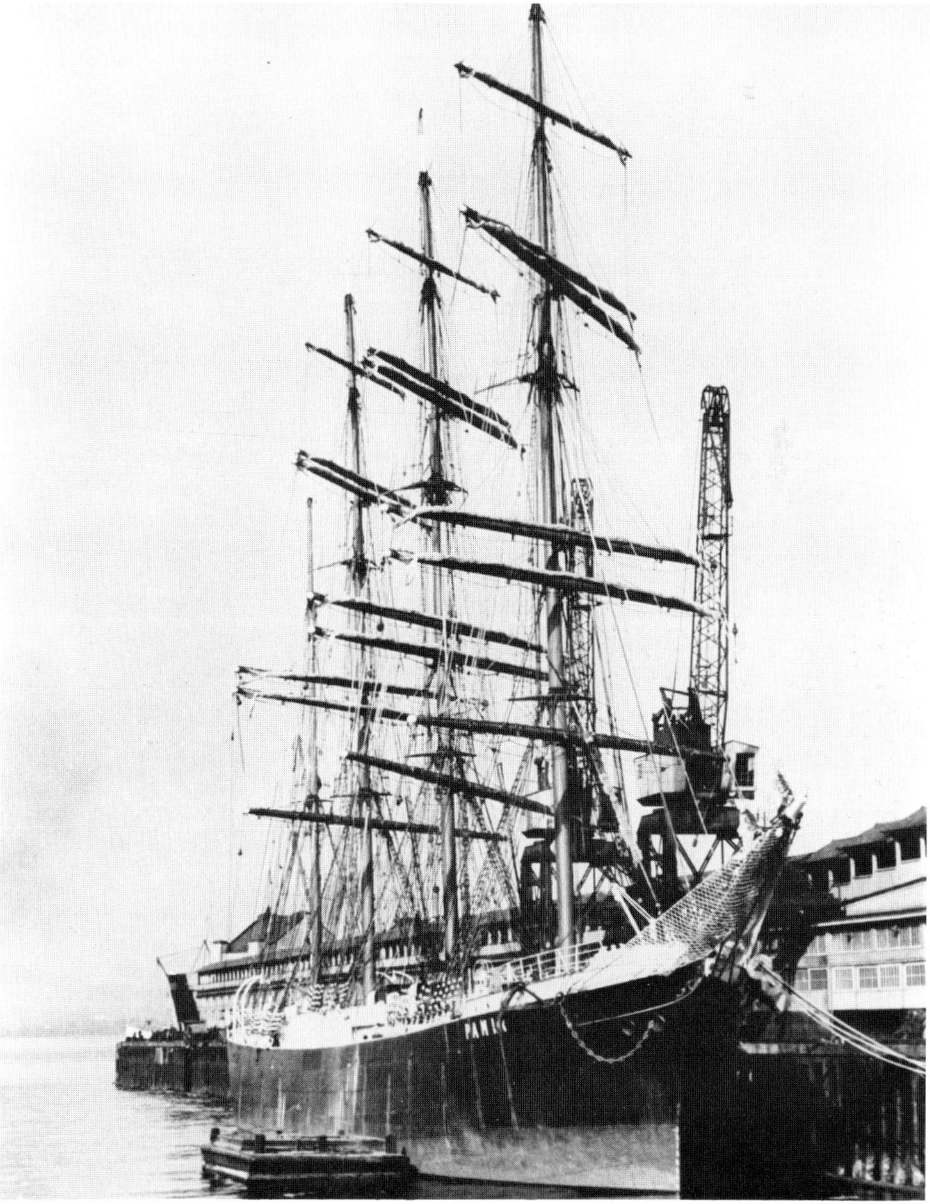

VMM

. . . *Pamir*

The *Pamir* at the North Vancouver Midland Pacific Terminal with the 1940s' Vancouver skyline in the background.

Pamir under tow in Juan de Fuca Strait. RCAF HSL (high-speed launch) and Canso aircraft in attendance.

The four-masted barque *Pamir* off Cape Flattery, 8 July 1945. An RCAF photograph taken from one of the Canso reconnaissance aircraft based at BR4 Ucluelet Station, Vancouver Island.

It was not all play, however, as there was plenty to do in readying the ship for the return part of the voyage. The *Pamir* was moved to the grain wharf at North Vancouver (Midland Pacific) where she loaded 3,500 tons of bagged wheat which brought the ship down to her marks, drawing 23 feet 11 inches aft.

It is interesting to note that while the *Pamir* was in Vancouver on this first Canadian visit, she was, on 15 June, finally condemned as a prize. The New Zealand government had decided to secure this final condemnation, thus taking title to the vessel. The interim order which had placed the ship under possession of the Crown, was automatically superseded (legal proceedings had arisen out of that first seizure in 1941 which were subsequently discontinued when a second seizure and release to the Crown were effected).

The ship then had become a New Zealand vessel, but there was still a legal problem which prevented her being registered as a New Zealand vessel due to her title being invested in the Crown – the court could not legally decide to which country of His Majesty the vessel should belong (New Zealand or the United Kingdom). The continuing matter of using the *Pamir* as a training ship was still receiving strong consideration in New Zealand at this time.

On 7 July, the tug *Island Commander* again came alongside the *Pamir* in the still of an early summer morning. The ship was eased out into the stream where she anchored to await the tide at the First Narrows (Lions Gate) Bridge. Then at 10:00 a.m. her official departure from Vancouver was recorded as the tow headed for the open sea. By late afternoon of the 8th, the tow had passed Victoria, dropped the pilot, and was well down the Strait and pitching gently into the incoming westerly swells of the open Pacific. Fog had persisted in the Strait but fortunately cleared off by the time the tow reached the open ocean.

By late afternoon, the tow had cleared Swiftsure and was proceeding to a good offing and finally, when about 40 miles off Cape Flattery, with a good northwest breeze, the tug was slipped at 7:00 p.m. Many beautiful photos of the *Pamir* were obtained during these moments by B. G. (Gordon) Moodie, now deceased, who went on the *Island Commander* specifically for the purpose of recording this event. As an amateur photographer who took great interest in the *Pamir* while she was in Vancouver, he and his family became great friends of the crew. He took many photos from all parts of the ship, even from up in the royal rigging, and when the ship's newspaper, *Pamir Press*, came out during the voyage home, there was special mention for Flight Sergeant Moodie of the RCAF Marine Division, whose fine photographs eventually ended up as prize possessions of many of the *Pamir* men in New Zealand and elsewhere and certainly, any publication about the *Pamir* thereafter always featured one or more of the Moodie photos.

After a couple of days in light airs and fog off the American coast, during which time aircraft had often flown overhead, the ship finally broke into the clear allowing the aerial visitors to obtain photos. The ship, with better winds, was able to stand well clear from the land. On one occasion, while sailing in fog, an American destroyer suddenly appeared just as the boys were having their tea – they came out on deck and watched while the destroyer circled them, even training its guns, presumably in practise, on the *Pamir*. Apparently, on an earlier voyage outbound from San Francisco, they were similarly intercepted by a U.S. ship which repeatedly challenged them for identification.

The *Pamir Press* made further reference to their Vancouver visit. The Vancouver press had been given the freedom of the ship but it was felt that it had been written up poorly. There was also mention of promised photos to the crew for their help and services rendered, and further mention of their being charged 50 cents for photos. The Canadian press had not met with any great favour as far as the Kiwi crew was concerned.

The *Pamir Press* was an interesting little publication which had been produced entirely aboard the ship during passage. It helped make the voyages interesting for the crew. As well as contributions of various topics from different crew members, there was usually some comment on such occasions as crossing the "Line," deck game participation, and world and war news.

The *Pamir* crossed the equator 24 days out on this southbound voyage and made her New Zealand landfall on 25 August after sailing 6,606 miles in 48 days and 23 hours – her fastest time across the Pacific – a very creditable run which greatly pleased her captain and crew. Captain A. R. Champion left the *Pamir* after this voyage to resume his duties as pilot at Lyttelton in New Zealand. The ship's official arrival at

Wellington was recorded on 28 August, giving a total passage time of 52 days. Captain Champion signed off the ship on 12 September.

When all the receipts and disbursements for the voyage had been accounted, the net result showed a profit, but only some £2,000 which was far from the profit figures of the earlier San Francisco voyages. This figure was later revised to a profit of £3,800.

It was decided to send the *Pamir* again to Vancouver for another cargo of wheat.

The *Pamir* tows out under Lions Gate Bridge.

Island Commander . . . alongside

. . . standing by

. . . and departing, Vancouver Harbour.

... Lions Gate, astern.

Tow passsing under Lions Gate bridge

The *Pamir* heads into the Strait of Georgia.

The North Shore Mountains and Point Grey, astern.

Rounding East Point for Boundary Pass

Pamir makes sail.

. . . and into Juan de Fuca Strait.

Pamir fills away.

Bon voyage

. . . New Zealand bound.

The routes of the *Pamir* tows showing frequently mentioned place names.

Pamir meets *Island Warrior* off Cape Flattery.

THE SECOND VANCOUVER VOYAGE

The *Pamir*'s seventh voyage, and second one to Vancouver, commenced on 22 September 1945 under a new master, Captain D. C. Champion, brother of the former master. He signed on the ship on 13 September. The crew this time contained many new faces and numbered 40 New Zealanders in the total. D. W. Galloway was first mate, and had missed the previous voyage in order to sit for his Mate's ticket, having served as second mate on the San Francisco voyages. His experience in sail dated back into the 1930s when he started out as a deck boy on one of the Erikson sailing ships. Andy Keyworth was again second mate and Mr. Francis Renner the third mate. There were two extra deck boys taken on this voyage.

Since VJ Day (Victory over Japan, 14 August) had occurred during the last southbound voyage from Vancouver, there was then much more publicity given to the *Pamir* in the New Zealand press – hostilities and secrecy then having ceased. The ship's name was once more painted on her side and again loaded with tallow (approximately 1,100 tons), she made a long run of six weeks to the equator. When the ship passed within radio contact of Pitcairn Island, the Islanders indicated that if the *Pamir* passed close on its next voyage and had anything for them, they would come off in their boats. The *Pamir* then tracked northward picking up the southeast trades and later, because of calms and currents, was carried close to the Marquesas Islands before getting through the doldrums and into the northeast trades.

The ship's second approach to Cape Flattery and the Juan de Fuca Strait was made in late November in conditions far different from the first approach the previous summer. Of the three voyages that the *Pamir* made to our waters, this second voyage is the most memorable because of the conditions the ship met off Cape Flattery when both inbound and outbound. The descriptions of her arrival and departure on this voyage really showed the dangers that sailing ship masters faced when approaching the entrance adjacent to the dangerous lee shore of Vancouver Island between Cape Beale and Carmanah Point. And when one considers that mariners of earlier times did not have the advantage of modern aids like radio and direction-finding bearings for position, or even lights as navigation aids, the experiences of the *Pamir* on this occasion even further emphasize the reasons why the west coast of Vancouver Island was known as the "graveyard" of ships.

The *Pamir* encountered bad weather as she tracked northward off the American coast and gradually closed Cape Flattery. Bill Galloway, first mate, and Larkin Healy, radio officer, both remembered only too well that period of bad weather as they approached their landfall. They had not had any sights for days in the thick weather. When close enough to the land, they were able to obtain DF bearings from American coast stations but were unable at first to obtain the necessary intersecting bearings

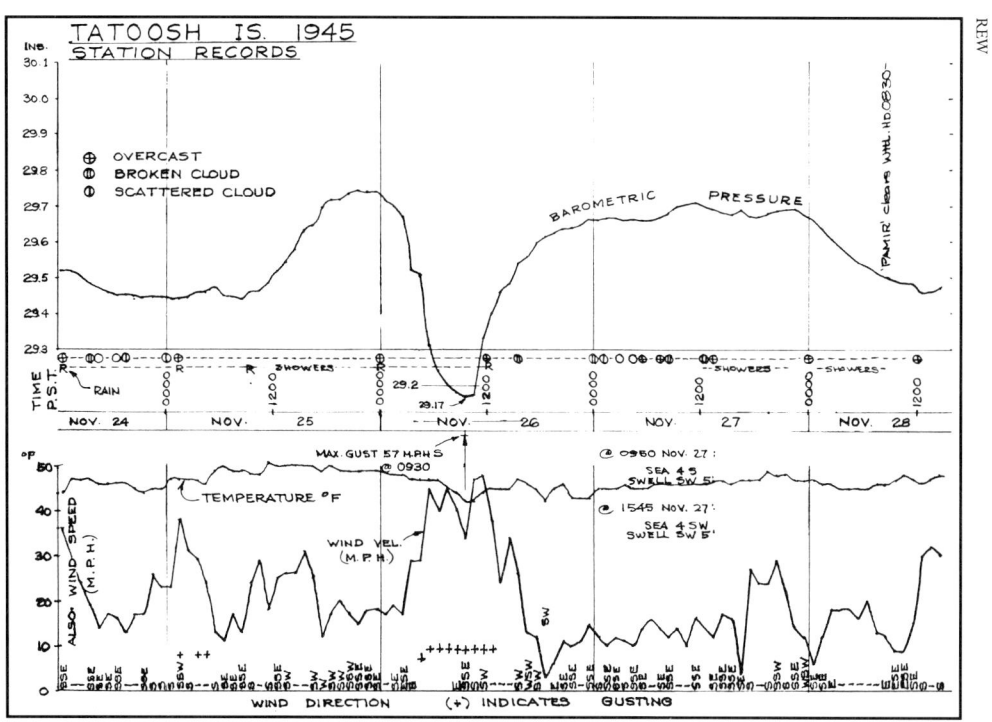

Figure 1, Tatoosh Island 1945, Station Records.

from the Canadian stations as they got further northward. So they could not accurately establish their position fix when they really needed it.

As the *Pamir* approached the coast, the weather remained thick with rain throughout these late November days, which were noticeably shorter and colder. The weather records from Tatoosh Island (Figure 1) for the period 24 to 28 November give a clear indication of the situation as the *Pamir* entered the area. Entries from the captain's report, written upon completion of the voyage, dramatically emphasize the concern, quick decisions required, and the feel of impending conditions which the master had to be able to assess and thus ensure the safety of his ship and crew.

The following entries, read in conjunction with the data shown in Figure 1, will clearly indicate the situation off Cape Flattery.

> 23 November: Wind fresh northwest. Set course for Swiftsure. Advising position by radio.
>
> 23 November: Midnight. Wind changed southwest 5-7. Making good time – average 8 knots. ETA Swiftsure 2300 hours 25th.

Throughout the 24th, the ship continued on her northward course. On Sunday afternoon, the 25th, the ship stood in towards Cape Flattery with a fair wind from the southwest. At about 2230 hours the landfall was made with Tatoosh light coming into view. Via radio, a rendezvous had already been arranged with the tug *Island Warrior* which was steaming outbound to meet the *Pamir*.

But at midnight, after the barometer had risen throughout most of the day, it started to fall and the wind had backed into the southeast. In radio-telephone conversations between the tug and the ship, the tug skipper gave warning of the Sunday forecast which indicated strong southeast winds – this forecast soon became fact. The master's entries continue:

> 25 November: Midnight. Wind increased southeast. Reduced sail.
>
> 26 November: 0100 hours. Pachena Point bearing 060° 22 miles. Immediately headed ship out to sea. Down to upper and lower topsails. Making 8 knots. Barometer falling rapidly.
>
> 0400. Wind southeast 9. Continued to claw away from the land.
>
> 0800-0830. Barometer steady 29.13. Watching for wind change. Wind shift southwest 8. Put ship on starboard tack and hove to.

0900-1000. Wind southwest 10-11. Barometer rising rapidly. Ship handling well.

1200. Wind west southwest 7.

1600. Wind west southwest 3. High seas and heavy swell. Position 55 miles off Swiftsure. Bearing 072°. Communicated with tug *Island Warrior*. Asked conditions in Strait. Reply "Too tough out here for me. Captain, stay out until daybreak."

The tug, en route to Swiftsure, was having a hard time of it and was forced to turn back. It would have been impossible to pass a towline in the prevailing conditions. The radio-telephone conversations between the sailing ship's master and the towboat skipper told the story and they agreed to make a meet when conditions were more favourable, hopefully the next morning.

Inspection of the Tatoosh Island records shows that, just at about 0930 hours, a maximum windspeed gust of 57 m.p.h. occurred. The barometer had bottomed out and a wind veer came quickly into the southwest as the front went through. The Victoria evening paper that day reported on the storm – which did a lot of damage in the area – and the local meteorological station reported peak velocity of 58 m.p.h. at about the same time as Tatoosh Island.

Out where the *Pamir* was, the winds were estimated at Force 10-11 with a maximum of about 75 m.p.h. – hurricane force. The sea around the ship was described as white. The mate recalled, "It blew like hell, and with the ship reduced to just her lower topsails, we just hung on, hove to." The ship had great strength and had endured such conditions many times before.

The worst of the short but violent storm was over. The ship beat back and forth offshore for the remainder of that day. The "graveyard" to leeward had been avoided. By the time darkness had set in, the barometer had shown a good recovery and the winds had dropped to a breeze. But the storm had left heavy seas in its wake.

27 November: 0600. Wind southwest 4-5. Making 7-8 knots. Checking position hourly

0900. Indication more southeast weather. Communicated with tug. Come out immediately. Bearing 062° 40 miles off Swiftsure.

1300. Sighted tug. Taking in sail. Heaving ship to.

1330. Tug standing by.

1400. Towline aboard.
1410. Tow commenced.

The example dramatically illustrated how quickly conditions could change in the area and how a ship could be caught unless every precaution was taken. And, even then, many a ship's master stood helplessly on his ship's deck, as it was unavoidably carried shoreward in the grip of the dangerous currents. Under such storm conditions and at a time of flood tide, the prevailing north-setting current off the coast can attain a speed of over three knots off the general area of the Strait entrance. Such conditions have been the cause of many, many shipwrecks on the outer west coast of Vancouver Island over the years.

Radio officer Healy was on duty day and night during that period as DF bearings were continuously being obtained and contact with shore stations maintained. In fact, he recalled having to use wet sacks to try to keep the alternators cooled because of the heat generated from almost continuous transmitter operation. The radio room on the *Pamir* was beneath the chart room on the midships structure. There was a steady stream of messages and bearings being passed back and forth between these two rooms that stormy night and day off Vancouver Island. Mate Galloway recalled that it was a dirty time and that they were well aware of that lee shore – "we had a difficult time making our landfall that trip and then with the storm on top of that, we were kept pretty busy!"

After the tow had commenced, the mates commented that the skipper of the tug had done a fine job in getting out to them and moreover, he had handled that little craft like a wizard in the nasty sea still running. The tug skipper so complimented was Charlie Goodwin, now deceased, and a well-known skipper at the time in local towboating.

The master of the *Pamir* communicated with the tug every hour as the tow proceeded in and advised that all was OK.

27 November: 1815. Swiftsure abeam. Proceeding in. Wind change southeast 4-5.
2045. Tatoosh abeam.
28 November: 0640. Cleared Race Rocks.
0800. Pilot, Port Doctor, Customs boarded.
0830. Pratique granted. Tow transferred to tug *Robert Preston*.

2220. Cleared Lions Gate.
2240. Let go towline.
2320. Making fast at berth.
29 November: 0030. All secure.

So ended the second northbound voyage to Vancouver. Many articles in various newspapers, both in Canada and New Zealand, and elsewhere, gave details about the gale off Cape Flattery and the *Pamir*'s close call off the west coast of Vancouver Island. And there was creditable mention of the tug which finally got out to pick up the ship off Swiftsure. Some of the reports were perhaps over-dramatized. There was great interest in the appearance of such a ship as the *Pamir* in these waters at a time when it had become a rarity. Indeed, the men aboard the *Pamir* were happy to finally be under tow that day – they knew that it was no place for a sailing ship to be when not in tow with the shore only a few miles to leeward and indications of another southeaster setting in.

The tug *Island Warrior* was a sister ship of the *Island Commander*, both vessels having been built as North Sea trawlers. However, the *Warrior* had not been converted to diesel as the *Commander* had been, and she still had her triple expansion steam engine, and except for the hull was entirely different in appearance from her sister ship.

Aboard the *Pamir* that day, all sail was furled and the gaskets passed around them on the yards. The men on the yards were more used to the warmer and tropical winds blowing from behind them; that day, while towing up the Strait into the easterly weather, was recalled as being cold and unpleasant. Late November in the Pacific northwest was a far cry from balmier conditions of lower latitudes and following breezes. Mate Galloway recalled the cold that day. Radio officer Healy said he hit his bunk as soon as they got tow – it had been a trying 48 hours for him and his assistant radio officer. It will be recalled that the war with Japan was over and on this voyage all the DF workings and other transmissions were not carried out in code, so that, at least, made those moments easier for the radiomen.

After the tow cleared William Head, the former quarantine station for trans-Pacific liners, the Straits Towing Company's tug *Robert Preston* took over the tow from that point with a pilot on board, and the *Pamir* was once more taken through the Gulf Islands to her arrival at Vancouver late that evening where she berthed at the CPR pier.

The official end of the voyage was logged as 28 November with the ship having sailed a distance of 8,991 miles in 67 days and 4 hours – an average speed of 5.6 knots. Again, a cargo of tallow was discharged and the ship was shifted to the grain wharf (Midland Pacific) at North Vancouver. She commenced loading her wheat cargo on 7 December.

There was the usual round of socializing. This time crew members skated on Lost Lagoon, instead of swimming in English Bay. During a part of the ship's stay, everything was iced up for awhile and decks froze over as soon as water was put to them. It was Christmas in Vancouver – an elaborate menu was prepared by the ship's cook, but many of the crew were entertained on shore. A souvenir Christmas menu was lightheartedly drawn up by the energetic Mr. Moodie, the photographer, and the cook, who superimposed a menu over a photo of the *Pamir* under full sail off Cape Flattery which he had taken during last summer's visit.

There were many other memories involving escapades of the crew while the ship was in Vancouver: the girls at the grain wharf, the visit of the brewery people aboard and the return visit to the plant and the sampling of the product, serenading one of the mate's girlfriends, the Doctor and the Bishop, a ride in an ambulance, the Wrens . . . many memories! But again, it wasn't all play, and there was much to do aboard ship in readiness for the return voyage and much of the gear was overhauled.

On 20 December the loading of bagged wheat had been completed, with approximately 3,600 tons aboard. The following day the *Pamir* was shifted away from the wharf to be moored to dolphins and well secured in the event of any strong westerly winds. On 5 January lines were singled up in preparation for taking tow. At 0800 that morning a towline from the tug *Snohomish* was taken on board and the tow for the open ocean commenced.

0900. Lions Gate Bridge cleared.

2045. Pilot dropped.

2215. Race Rocks abeam. Weather fine, clear. Moderate northwest 4.

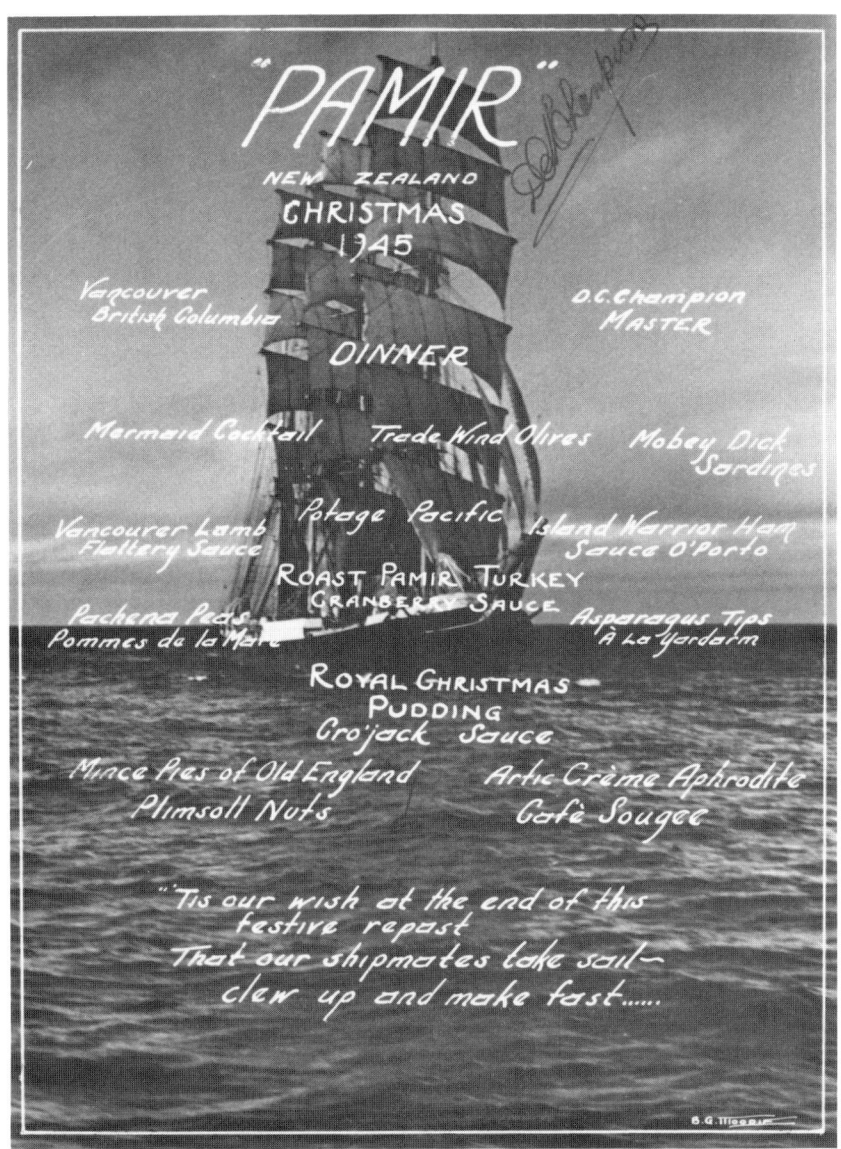

Christmas Dinner Menu, onboard *Pamir*, December 1945.

Pamir

New Zealand

Vancouver Christmas D. C. Champion
British Columbia 1945 Master

DINNER

Mermaid Cocktail	Trade Wind Olives	Moby Dick Sardines
Vancouver Lamb Flattery Sauce	Potage Pacific	Island Warrior Ham Sauce O'Porto
Pachena Peas Pommes de la Main	Roast Pamir Turkey Cranberry Sauce	Asparagus Tips à la Yardarm
Mince Pies of old England Plimsoll Nuts	Royal Christmas Pudding Cro'jack Sauce	Arctic Crème Aphrodite Café Sougée

'Tis our wish at the end of this
festive repast
That our shipmates take sail –
clew up and make fast . . .

The veteran tug *Snohomish,* of ex-U.S. Coast Guard fame and also owned by the Island Tug and Barge Limited, was a powerful vessel and her acquisition by the Canadian towing company along with other acquisitions of ex-U.S. Army tugs, gave that firm one of the largest and most powerful fleets of towing boats on the coast. Old *Sno,* as she was affectionately known to those who served aboard her, towed all that day through the Gulf Islands. The Moodies watched her that morning while the tow proceeded past Point Grey in a stiff breeze. The weather appeared to be improving. Under cloud and calm conditions the barometer continued to rise. Shortly after midnight, however, the barometer began to fall and by daylight when the tow had proceeded well into the Juan de Fuca Strait, the wind had come on strongly from the east. Here was the *Pamir* once more approaching the Cape Flattery region and the weather had turned for the worse. The *Snohomish* was making good time with the *Pamir* but it was getting dirty – it was raining and the wind continued to pick up and the barometer was then falling rapidly.

Following are entries from the reports by the *Pamir*'s master:

6 January: 0215. Communicated with tug. Ease up. Put extra preventer on towline inboard.

0820. Tatoosh abeam.

0900. Commenced setting sail. Southeast 6 and freshening.

1145. Let go tug. Heavy seas. Southeast 8. Rain. Position well clear of Swiftsure. Ran for it to sea – west southwest.

1155. Shipped a heavy sea aboard starboard bow. Lifted anchor. Dented badly plate in way of anchor bill. Secured under direction of mate. Unable to ship anchors inboard. Extra lashings. Shipping seas everywhere. Accommodations a shambles.

1800. Well clear of land. Rolling rails under.

These entries tell the story along with an inspection of the Tatoosh Island weather records for the period (Figure 2).

Mate Galloway remembered the tug towing like hell and they signalled *Snohomish* to slow down – they didn't want the towline to part – the way the weather was shaping up – especially being at such close quarters with the land. The radio telephone was getting a lot of use about this time and there was apparently some dispute between the master and the skipper of the tug about when to slip the tow.

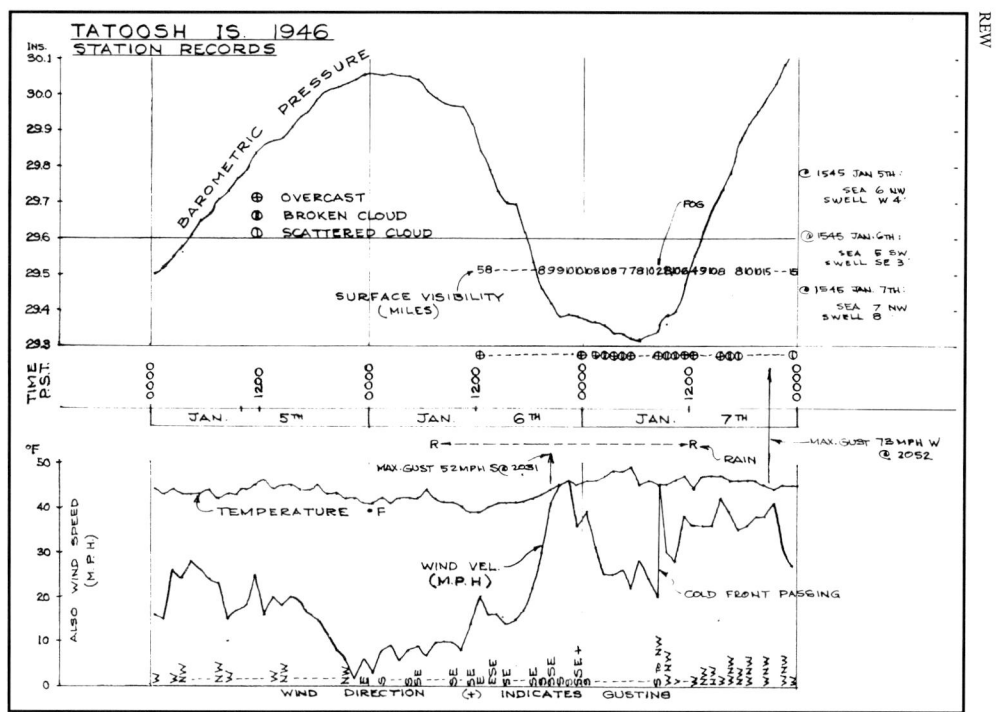

Figure 2, Tatoosh Island 1946, Station Records.

    As the tow neared the open sea the weather deteriorated rapidly – once more the *Pamir* was off Flattery. The winds had now reached gale force. But aside from the wind and the state of the sea which *Pamir* could easily take in its stride, a sign of danger was observed up forward where the towline had been made fast. The pennant securing the towline was chafing at the hawsepipe in the heavy going. If it was allowed to continue, the towing wire could part and in the prevailing conditions there would be little chance that the tug could pass another wire to them. With great difficulty, the wire was re-secured on a better lead. A decision had to be made quickly. It was decided to put sail on – they could not afford to take the chance of being caught near the Vancouver Island shoreline only a few miles off to starboard. By this time the tow was clear of the Strait entrance and heading into the open sea.

All hands were on deck aboard the *Pamir* now and orders sent men aloft to loosen gaskets – as each sail was set, the *Pamir*'s speed increased. With upper and lower topsails and inner jib and all four topmast staysails set, the ship came charging ahead overhauling the *Snohomish*. The towline was still intact. When the *Pamir* came up on the tug's quarter, the *Snohomish*'s skipper became rather anxious because the *Pamir* could have pulled old *Sno* around the way she was going.

The *Snohomish* had a flying bridge which was supported at the rail by stanchions and bracing. The tug was well heeled over by the lead of the towline over the counter as the *Pamir* came up on her. Seas were heavy then. The skipper told his mate to signal the *Pamir* to let go. That mate was Jim Talbott (he became Captain Talbott of other deep-sea tugs towing in the Pacific). He was able to brace himself among those stanchions under the flying bridge and make the signal ("better let go"). Talbott said the *Pamir* was almost abeam the tug with the bight of the towline before they let go.

Aboard the *Snohomish* at that time was the Vancouver photographer Norman MacNeil who had gone on this tow purposely to obtain photos of what was then thought to be the last time the *Pamir* would be seen in the area. What happened in those few minutes when the *Pamir* came racing up on the tug was beyond a photographer's dream: under very difficult conditions, he was able to obtain a series of photos of the *Pamir* in heavy weather under reduced sail that became famous throughout the world. Seldom was there a chance to photograph a ship such as this under such conditions. The *Pamir* came surging towards the *Snohomish* and literally roared past and faded into the darkness of the storm ahead. Others aboard the tug were also able to obtain photos of the sight.

The tow was slipped just before noon on 6 January 1946.

The words of those aboard the *Snohomish* at the time vividly described the scene:

> We witnessed a drama reminiscent of that age long past when clippers reigned supreme – as we stood spellbound, the *Pamir* came racing towards us. Huge seas boiled over her bow, her sails billowed out to the full, it was a scene of grandeur. Heeled well over in the terrific wind, she swept by majestically. *Snohomish*'s flags ran up spelling "Bon Voyage" and her steam whistle hooted farewell to one of the last great wind ships.

Some of Mr. MacNeil's photos of these moments were featured in the May 1948 edition of the *National Geographic* magazine and his entire series is featured here in the composite of the second Vancouver voyage.

The *Pamir* clawed away from the lee shore. Mate Galloway said that it was "chancy" that morning but they had no choice – they had to react quickly to a situation and make the right decision. Usually, when first setting sail on a voyage, care has to be taken to ensure that there were no "twisted clews" (in the case of the square sail the clews are the bottom corners to which the sheets, or controlling lines, are connected – if there is a twist in the sail corner when it is set, there can be great strain on the canvas in a blow and it can easily tear at this point). On this occasion there was not time to worry about twisted clews and the ship successfully stood out to sea on the port tack.

With the *Pamir* already obscured in the thick weather, the old *Snohomish* turned for home – she rolled her wheelhouse doors in the sea that day and they had water on the wheelhouse deck, an indication of the rough conditions. Dramatic words from those aboard the *Pamir* described the scene as *Snohomish* turned for home: "The *Snohomish* steaming away for Juan de Fuca – a fuss of white at his whistle and the international code signal streaming in the gale."

The *Pamir*'s paper recorded this Vancouver voyage as "experiencing a typical North American winter there including Cape Flattery as a prelude" – obviously referring to the stormy period when inbound. The *Pamir* made her New Zealand landfall on 12 March. She arrived in tow at Wellington the following day after having completed a passage of 7,166 miles in 65 days and 9 hours – an average speed of 4.5 knots. Her passage port to port was 68 days, the same time as her northward voyage to Vancouver.

Ten days out from Cape Flattery on this voyage home, on 16 January at 8:55 p.m. the cry of "man overboard" was heard. The ship was about 200 miles west of Cape Mendicino on the California coast. Ordinary seaman G. S. Gunn had fallen from the lee cross-jack yard arm. The ship was making little way fortunately, and he was able to work himself around to the rudder of the ship as it passed him, and there he hung on. The ship was hove to and mate Galloway went over the stern on a line and grabbed the boy as he swam to him. The pair were hoisted back on board over the counter and the ship resumed its course.

When the *Pamir* arrived back in New Zealand this time, she returned to increasing government concern for her future. Although her operation this far still showed a credit balance, the net returns of these later voyages were becoming less and less. She did, however, on this second Vancouver voyage, realize a profit of £3,100 – again a very small amount compared to her earnings of earlier voyages. Her receipts for freight northbound were £5,800 and southbound with the Canadian wheat, £21,800, giving a total income of £27,600. Against this were disbursements of some £24,500.

It was decided that the ship should make yet another voyage to Vancouver but the unavailability of cargo was becoming a serious problem. Careful consideration was given to the obtaining of a lumber cargo from Vancouver and New Westminster. Upon leaving New Zealand once more, it was planned that this latter commodity would be her southbound return loading.

The *Pamir* overhauls *Snohomish*.

Snohomish pulls the *Pamir* away from the jetty

. . . and the tow begins.

Departing from
Vancouver Harbour.

Pamir is approaching Lions Gate

Under tow in the Strait of Georgia.

. . . and passing Point Grey.

NMM

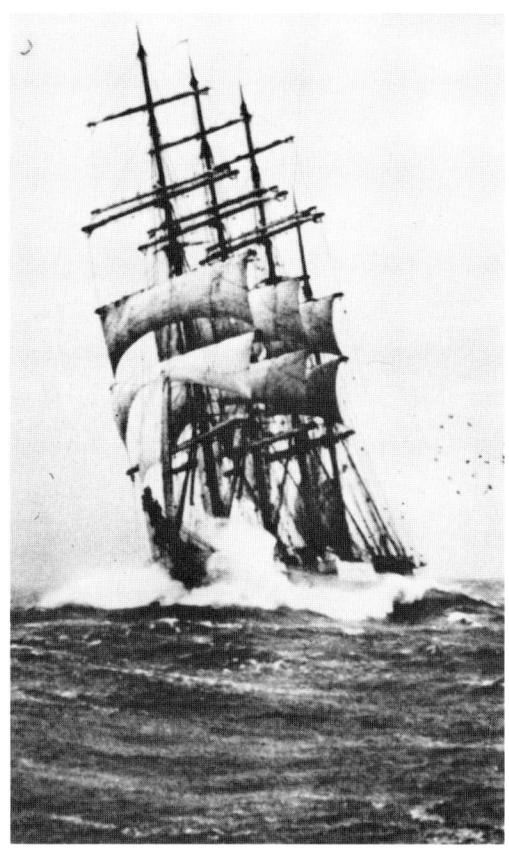

Still under tow, the *Pamir* overhauls *Snohomish*

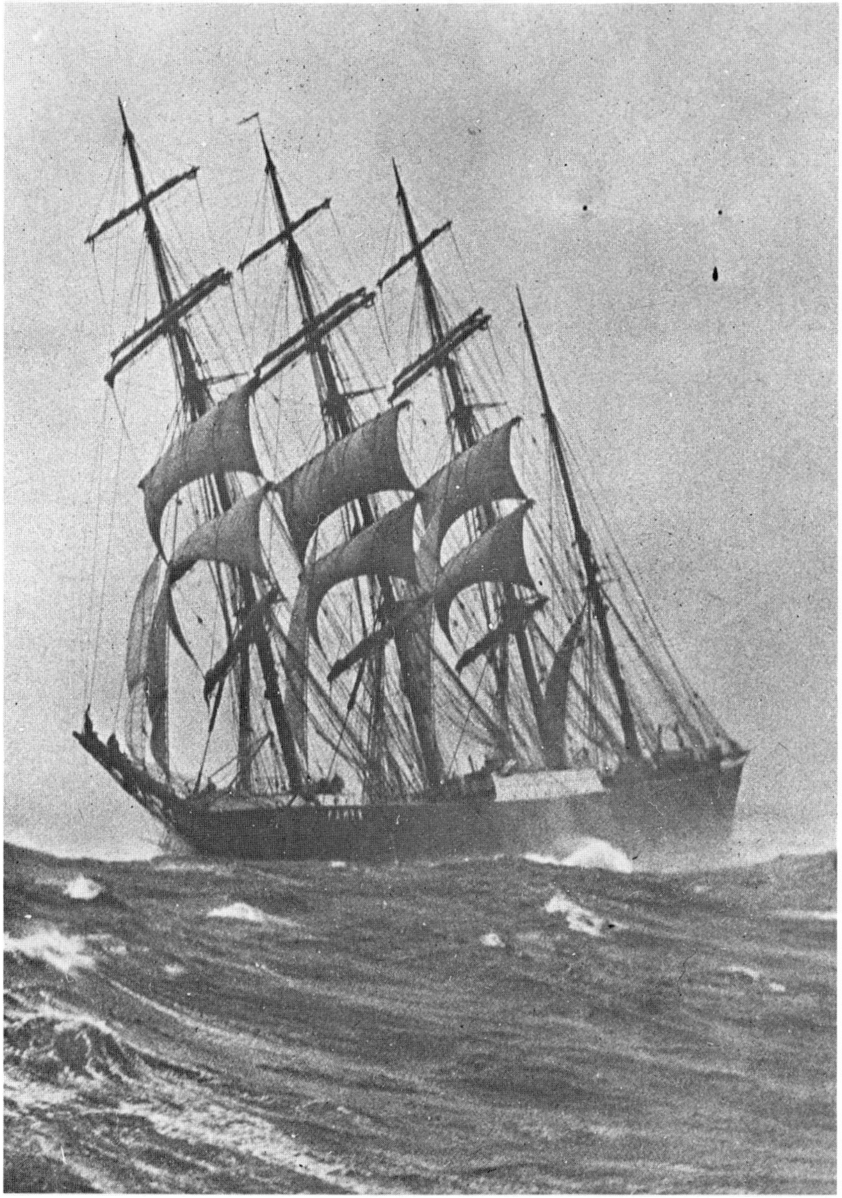

HF

. . . and charges ahead.

HF

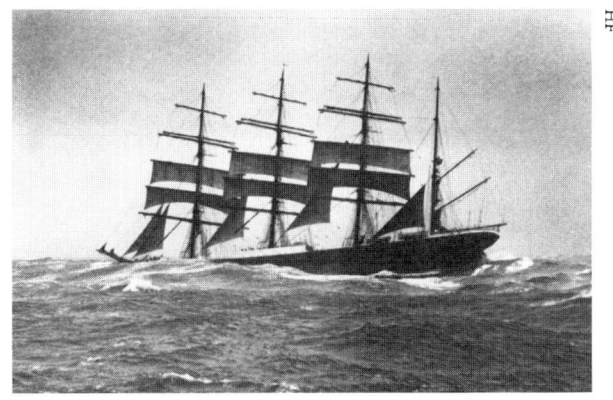

The *Pamir* free of her tow

NMM

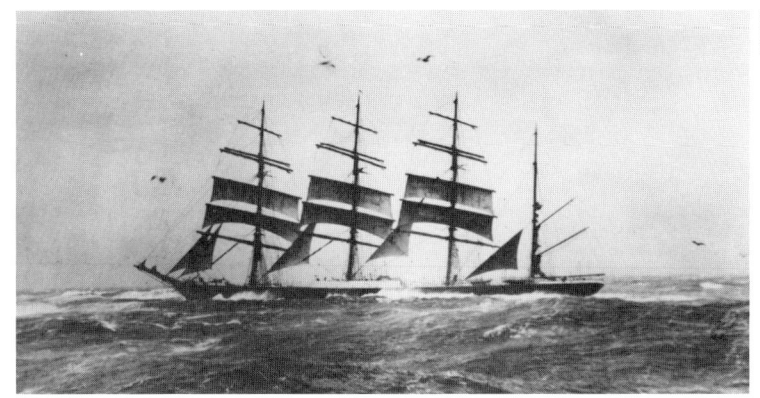

. . . surges past *Snohomish*

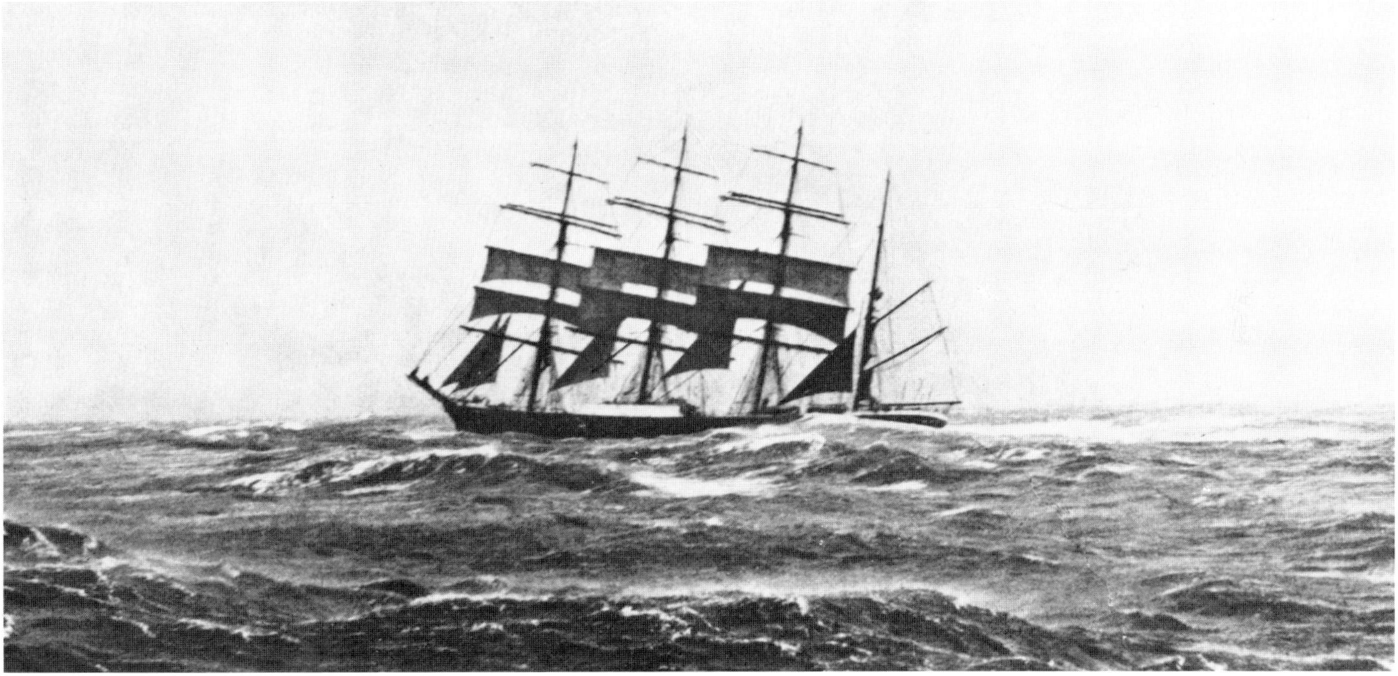

NMM

. . . and drives seaward into the storm.

The *Pamir* meets *Island Commander* off Cape Flattery.

THE THIRD VANCOUVER VOYAGE

The *Pamir* having been classed +100A1 by Lloyd's, again left Wellington with a part cargo of tallow (1,555 tons). The date was 5 May 1946. Captain D. C. Champion was again in command and there were many new faces in the crew. At the end of the previous voyage some crew members had been "sacked" and others "skinned out." The crew this time numbered 39 New Zealanders. Bill Galloway continued as first mate and Andy Keyworth second mate. There was a new third mate, A. F. Jenkins, who had come up through the ranks from deck boy on the *Pamir*, and who had missed the previous Vancouver voyage while he sat for his ticket. Mr. Healey was again the radio officer. In addition there was an assistant radio officer, the carpenter, the bosun and his mate, the sailmaker, and the motorman. There were 10 able seamen, 5 ordinary seamen and 15 deck boys plus the stewards and cooks, making up the complete crew, which was larger on this voyage.

Just before the *Pamir* sailed, authorization for a new suit of sails was granted by the government. The master had been dissatisfied with the American cotton sail canvas previously supplied at San Francisco and had requested a new suit of flax sail canvas from the United Kingdom similar to the pre-war sail supplied to the ship. It was arranged that these sails could be picked up in Vancouver.

The *Pamir* crossed the Line on 2 June and on this run carried well clear of Pitcairn Island, so the Islanders there did not get their chance to come off to the *Pamir*. On 15 June, after getting through the doldrums and up into the higher latitudes, the ship made a good run of 255 miles and afterwards averaged over 150 miles a day until she made her landfall. The ship's paper noted, after reference to the previous stormy arrival off Cape Flattery, "this time we shall see her [Vancouver] in all the glory of summer – a pleasant thought." On 29 June, the *Pamir* reported by radio that she was approximately 330 miles out from Cape Flattery and making 7 knots. It was expected that the ship would make Swiftsure by the 1st and accordingly a tug from Island Tug and Barge Ltd. was put on standby to make the rendezvous. The ship's log entries read as follows:

30 June 1946. Making 9 knots 133 miles to go.

1 July 0615. Both anchors put out and readied for taking tow.

1615. Sighted tug.

1800. Tug alongside but it was the *Island Commander*. 20 minutes to connect up [the indication here is that they expected the tug *Island Warrior*].

2100. Finished work. Under tow.

The *Pamir* was taken in tow by the *Island Commander* southwest of the Swiftsure Bank marker on 1 July. The ship had sailed 8,799 miles in 58 days and 8 hours, giving an average speed of 6.3 knots. She towed in under Lions Gate Bridge the following day. Her voyage was recorded as a 59-day passage. The ship arrived approximately at a time when Vancouver was a scene of much festivity, for it had been the first Dominion Day, the country's national holiday, since the end of the war.

The *Pamir*, under the New Zealand flag, was known as a ship that fed well, and certainly men like first mate Galloway, who had served aboard other ships in sail, knew this only too well. Unlike earlier-day sailing ships, the *Pamir* had been fitted with refrigeration equipment which had to have sufficient capacity to keep enough meat for over 40 men for 8 weeks or more. But the diesel compressors that had been installed gave a lot of trouble – the equipment as installed on a sailing ship which was always on a tack and listing one way or the other, raised "hell" with the engines. The equipment was repaired and serviced at Vancouver. There was trouble about the grub on this voyage and the cook and his assistant "skinned out" on arrival at Vancouver, in fact, it was said that they were ashore even before the ship's cat was! There were accusations that the cooks would let the bread rise for the officers but not even bother with this for the crew. With the prevailing feelings among the crew, it was just as well that the cooks jumped ship. One of the able seamen also left the ship this trip – he went ashore to marry the sister of a girlfriend of one of his shipmates – acquaintances that had been made on the previous voyages and visits to the grain wharf.

So, once again, the New Zealanders enjoyed themselves in the Vancouver summer. The ship's paper noted, "we once again created great interest as you all no doubt observed by the frequent invasions we suffered." While in Vancouver this time the ship had some minor repairs made on the bow plating due to damage caused by the anchor flukes in the previous stormy departure off Cape Flattery. The vessel was surveyed afloat on 11 July and to maintain her class was issued with a Lloyd's Certificate on the 17th after Burrard Shipyards had fitted doubling plates on both port and starboard bows.

This time, the *Pamir* was not taken over to the grain wharf after her cargo of tallow had been taken out, nor was she to load a lumber cargo that had originally been considered. A return cargo of coal had been arranged by the New Zealand government, and it was to be the first shipment of a 50,000-ton order as well as the first cargo of coal to be imported from North America. The coal, a high-grade type for steaming to be used by New Zealand Railways, was to come from the Cumberland mine on Vancouver Island and was to be loaded at the colliery wharf at Union Bay. This Comox hard coal was referred to by the whaling vessels in previous years when they bunkered there. It was described by them as really good steaming coal which the firemen on board the chaser boats liked because it involved a lot less work, and burnt slowly and hot, leaving little white ash and no cinders – it was the best coal you could get at the time.

And so, on 25 July, with a small amount of coal ballast on board, the *Pamir* was taken in tow by the Straits Towing Company tug *Robert Preston*. The ship was soon alongside at Union Bay after a relatively short tow across the Strait of Georgia. The *Pamir* loaded there until 2 August.

The crew's impression of Union Bay was not too complimentary but coal ports never were too appealing for the sailor. However, there was great interest in the ship and people came from far and near to view it. Many famous old sailing ships used to call at this very place in the heyday of the coal trade with California, and perhaps Donald MacKay's *Glory of the Seas* was the most noted. Now the *Pamir* was finally the last of the big wind ships to load there.

The crew had just a week to put in here. A pub was conveniently located – it is still there today but the wharf and facilities and most of the housing are all gone, the mines having closed down in 1953. There were dances ashore and visits to the mine, and there were recollections of the Chinese labourers working the cargo and finishing off.

On 3 August, the ship was ready for sea. She was loaded down to her marks with 3,474 tons, having a freeboard midships of 5 feet 8 inches. She was drawing 23 feet forward and 23 feet 11 inches aft and as such, was displacing approximately 6,500 tons. She was as deeply laden as she ever had been on her Canadian voyages. And so, with the pilot on board, on a beautiful and still summer morning, the *Pamir* was pulled away from the wharf out into the stream, and at noon, the tug *Island Warrior* came alongside and passed a towline which was hove aboard for the long tow to Cape Flattery. A new cook was aboard. The tow proceeded without incident until, in the morning of 5 August, the tug and its charge were well down the Juan de Fuca Strait and pitching into a westerly swell in light airs and fog. The heavily laden *Pamir* could just be seen slowly plunging up and down on the end of her towline. The *Island Warrior* towed on out past Cape Flattery in the fog and calm. Finally, after reaching a position about 45 miles southwest of Pachena Point, the fog lifted and a northwest breeze sprang up.

At 10:40 a.m. the tug raced forward – the *Pamir* had let go. Those aboard the tug didn't know it then, but this was the last time anybody would ever see the *Pamir* again in these waters. The *Island Warrior* swung around back towards the ship to watch her make sail. The crew on the *Pamir* could be seen quickly moving about the catwalks and into the rigging, letting go gaskets, hauling on halyards and manning braces. The ship made sail smartly and by noon had filled away on starboard tack with the wind on her quarter. The *Island Warrior* turned and went with her, but very soon the tug could no longer keep pace as the big ship gathered way. Parting blasts were then sounded on the tug's shrill steam whistle, everybody waved, and the little *Island Warrior* turned away, rolling northward back towards Vancouver Island. But all aboard the tug watched as the *Pamir* got smaller and smaller and was soon hull down on the horizon.

That was the last ever seen of the *Pamir* on the west coast of North America. On 12 August she logged her position as 28° 27′ N, 132° 27′ W, which put her approximately 1,500 miles south of Cape Flattery and well out to the southwest of Los Angeles. In seven days, she had made a creditable run, averaging over 200 miles a day. As she approached the low latitudes of the tropics, with the ensuing heat, the ventilation of the holds became of increasing importance with the coal cargo. Routine inspections of the cargo along with the usual fire and boat drills and pump checks were carried out and logged. The *Pamir* crossed the Line on the twenty-fourth day out.

After a week of strong westerly gales, the ship made her New Zealand landfall on 29 September and was taken in tow to arrive at Wellington harbour in the early hours of 1 October. The distance sailed was 6,972 miles in 56 days and 6 hours, giving an average speed of 5.2 knots. The voyage port to port was logged as 60 days. On this return voyage there had been ill feelings between crew and master, culminating in those last few stormy days before the landfall.

The *Pamir* was becoming of increasing concern – not only in regard to crew relations. It was known that this voyage would probably result in a loss, and there had been increased correspondence about new agreements with unions which was bound to have an effect on the operating expenses of the ship. As well, the cost of gear replacements and stevedoring expenses were continually escalating. When the figures were all tallied for this eighth voyage, the result was most discouraging. The *Pamir* had lost almost £18,000. Her expenses had risen on this voyage to a staggering £37,000 compared to the £24,500 of the previous Vancouver voyage. It was an expensive business to maintain such a well-found ship as the *Pamir*, especially in modern times, to the highest classification at Lloyd's, and the figures showed why the sailing ship became so scarce on the high seas after 1930 – it just could not compete with the modern steamship. A further breakdown of the voyage figures showed a northbound freight (tallow) receipt of £5,500. The coal freight realized £13,700, giving a total income of £19,200.

Word came back to Canada that the Comox coal was satisfactory for railway use. But the barque *Pamir* would not be making further voyages to North America.

It had become increasingly evident since her third voyage to San Francisco that obtaining cargo to North America was difficult, involving only part cargoes northbound; with southbound cargoes being bulk cargo, low freight earnings resulted, coupled with higher insurance rates. And, shippers preferred speedier delivery.

The *Pamir* in tow of *Island Warrior*.

The *Pamir* emerges from the fog.

The *Pamir* alongside at Union Bay

... loaded and prepared to depart

... *Island Warrior* standing by.

NMM

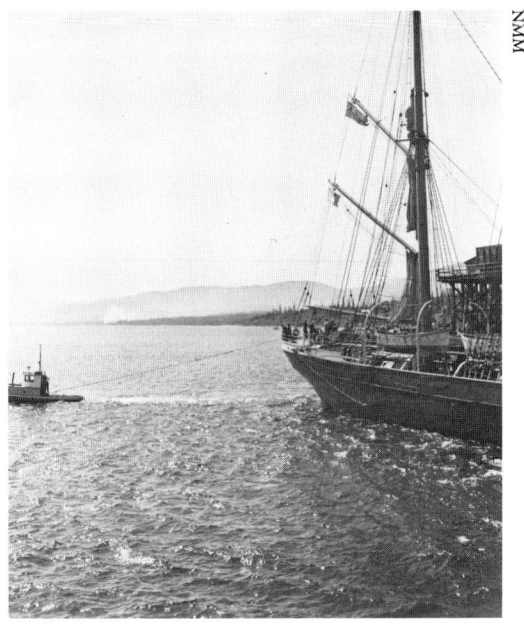

The stern is pulled away from the jetty

CDHS

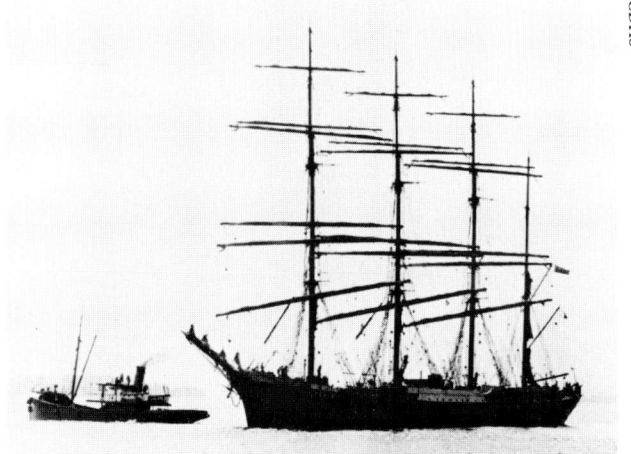

. . . *Island Warrior* ready to pass towline

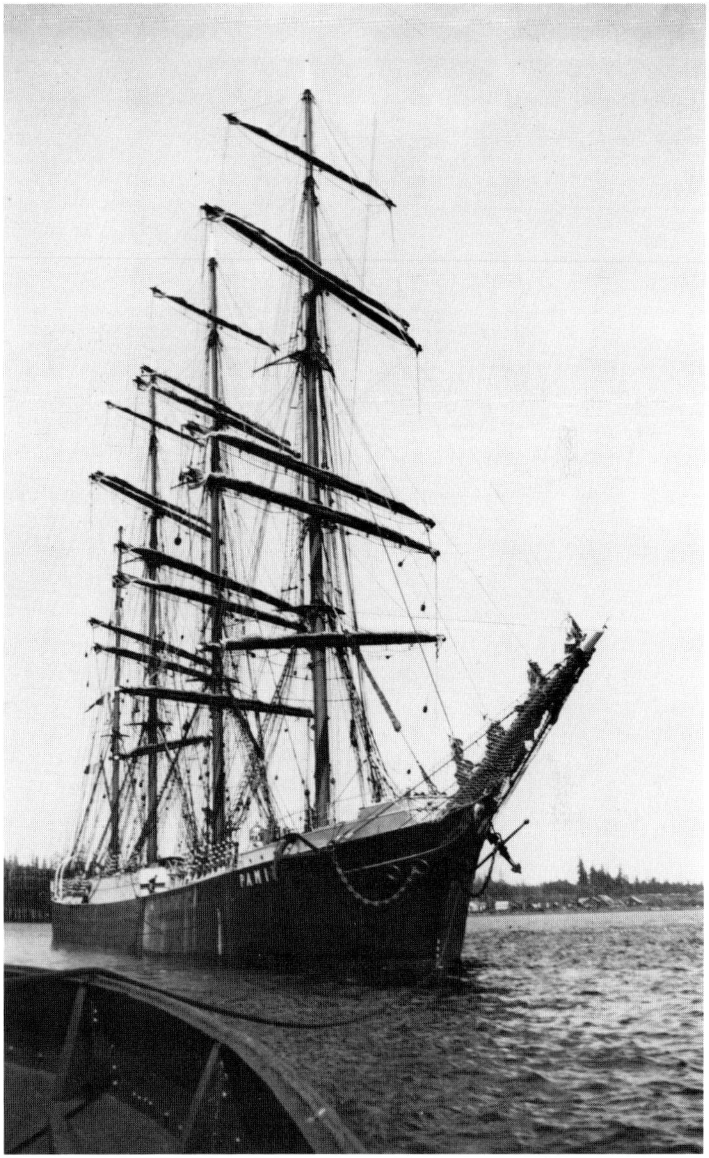

REW

. . . and the towline is connected.

The tow begins

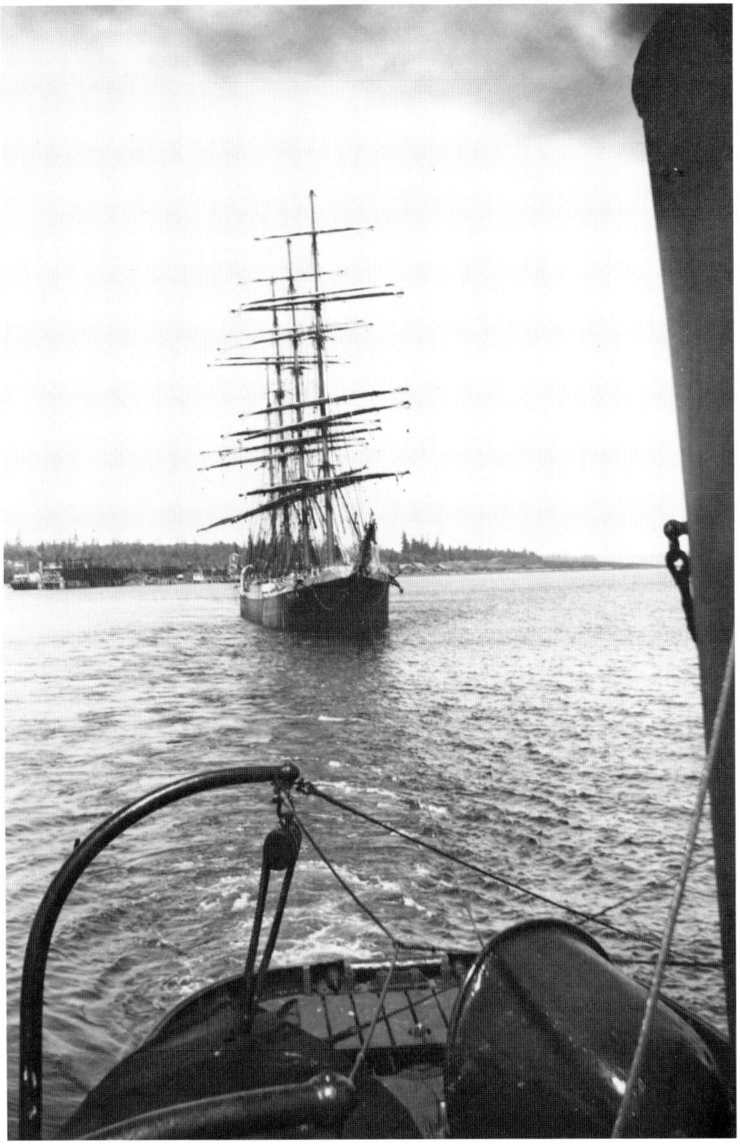
REW

NMM

. . . with Union Bay astern

. . . and into Baynes Sound.

NMM

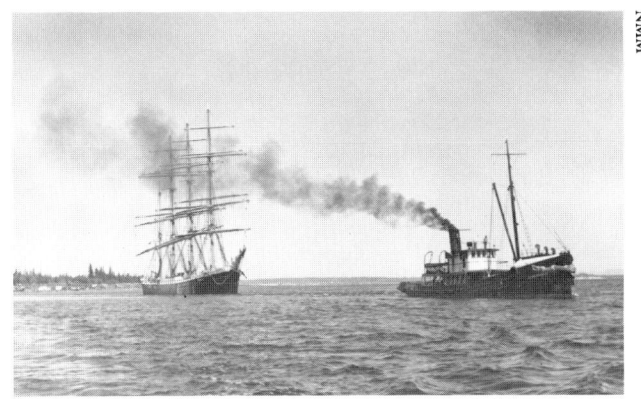

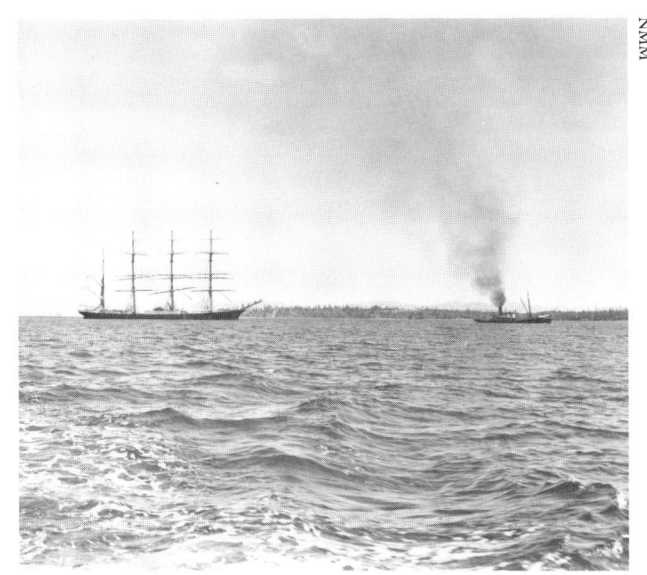

The *Pamir* makes sail off Cape Flattery

. . . gathers way

. . . and is Wellington, N.Z., bound.

Farewell *Pamir*.

AFTER THE VANCOUVER VOYAGES

The economics of the *Pamir*'s operation in the light of the loss that had been sustained on the last Vancouver voyage was under constant review by the New Zealand government. There was a tremendous public feeling for the ship in New Zealand and any suggestion of retiring her would have met with strong disfavour. Although the future operation of the ship would inevitably incur further loss, the government announced that the barque would continue in service only a few days after her arrival in Wellington. The ship then made another voyage, a relatively short one, to Australia, and the result was another £18,000 loss after her arrival back in Wellington in April 1947.

News that the *Pamir* was losing money soon reached many parts of the world, and offers to purchase her came from various locations amid strong representations from the New Zealand public to keep her at all costs – either in trade or as a training ship. Among proposals that came in at the time was a comprehensive scheme to purchase and operate the *Pamir* under a Commonwealth training organization. All such proposals were very confidential. This Commonwealth training scheme was of particular interest to Canadians, for it originated in British Columbia and was presented by the Canadian Shipping Company Ltd. of Vancouver in November of 1946, while the *Pamir* was loading for a voyage to Australia. Another proposal was received at Wellington that involved the ship's use in a publicity film for New Zealand made by the J. Arthur Rank orgainization.

The government was hard pressed by such communications to give a decision in the knowledge that the ship was now daily losing money. The government considered using the ship as a combined training ship and commercial carrier and continued to review the situation. Another letter came in from Canada regarding the Commonwealth training proposal. The original Canadian proposal, although declined, stirred the government departments concerned to conduct a detailed financial analysis of the ship's operation under the New Zealand flag, and the Secretary of the Treasury Department forwarded a full report to the External Affairs Department so that the matter of selling the *Pamir* could be further considered. The report explained that the most recent voyages of the ship had resulted in considerably reduced profits and finally losses, because of the dearth of suitable cargoes and in particular the outward cargoes. The large profits of earlier voyages had resulted from the selectivity of cargoes, with dangerous cargoes at double rates. However, merchants were reluctant to ship cargoes by this type of ship due to the time taken and the uncertainty involved, thus making it difficult for them to meet their markets. The report went on to explain that, on the other hand, strong representations from many masters and the public-at-large were made to use the *Pamir* as a training ship. The installation of small diesel engines to obviate towage and expedite arrivals was also considered, and in this regard the government had tried to obtain the plans of the ship from her original German builders in Hamburg, but they had been destroyed in Allied bombing raids. The report concluded that all factors considered, a reply to the Canadian proposal should indicate that the New Zealand government was not interested in the sale of the vessel. The appropriate reply was sent to Canada long before the *Pamir* came back from her Australian voyage to show her second large loss.

Before the ship came home from Australia, another query came in about her possible sale, this time from the United States. And in New Zealand, there was a suggestion to rename the ship with a Maori name. By June of 1947 the matter was still under consideration, but by the end of July the government made the difficult decision and announced that approval had been given to place the *Pamir* on voyage to the United Kingdom. In general, the announcement was received happily by the public and certainly by those who would have the chance to sign on for the voyage. But even amid the great publicity about this forthcoming voyage, there still came proposals for her purchase or other use, including participation in centennial celebrations and further opportunities in film-making.

After her arrival from the Australian voyage, the ship had incurred a further expenditure of some £7,000 during the five-month layup that followed before the decision was made to place her on yet another voyage. Such costs included, as well as the usual gear replacements and repairs, the cost of the annual survey and docking.

So the *Pamir* sailed early in October 1947 with wool and tallow for London and as she was en route, further communications came in from Europe about her sale.

After her much-publicized arrival in London, the Swedish government expressed an interest in her purchase. The communications never stopped coming in after the big loss was incurred on the last Vancouver voyage, and it seemed to the prospective purchasers at least, that sooner or later the New Zealand government would have to give up the ship. The government could not go on justifying repeated losses at the taxpayers' expense.

The *Pamir* was towed over to Antwerp and came home to New Zealand east-about with a mixed cargo. While en route homeward, another proposal was received at Wellington, this time for the ship to appear at Tahiti in a joint London-Hollywood production. The matter of charter was communicated and a rate of £160 a day was quoted plus the cost of ballasting the ship. However, the government would not indicate any definite disposition of the ship even after her expected arrival. The *Pamir* arrived at Auckland in late August 1948.

But during this U.K. voyage, the first thoughts of returning the ship to her former Finnish owners were aired in the government departments concerned. While she was en route home from Antwerp, what was probably one of the last, if not the last of the queries about her purchase, came from Nanaimo, British Columbia. A towing firm there was interested in her – for the lowly fate of becoming a barge. All of these proposals and queries about the ship and its future were, of course, unknown at the time, except to the parties and the government directly involved and as such, all considerations were held in the strictest confidence. Now, so many years later, it is interesting to learn that both the first and last of such proposals originated in British Columbia, Canada, where if only briefly, the *Pamir* had become so well known.

The future of this great ship had to soon be decided. The U.K. return voyage had resulted in a loss of £10,000. There had been more enquiries about her charter by the time she arrived back in Wellington on 1 October 1948, but just before this, on 24 September, the government finally made its decision and dispatched a cable to the the New Zealand High Commissioner in London who advised the Minister for Finland there indicating that the ship would be returned to that country. There was no way that the government could justify continued operation of the ship at a loss, either in commercial trade or as a training ship. An estimate of £50,000 a year was given as the amount required to operate her as a training vessel. However admirable the concept was, it simply was not possible to put her into this type of service in order to train a few lads.

The crew was paid off, and on 12 November, the ship was handed over to the Finnish representative at Wellington. There was a ceremony as the New Zealand flag came down and the Finnish flag was hoisted to the spanker gaff. With the majority of her crew made up of New Zealanders, the former Finnish master took the *Pamir* out of Wellington for the last time on 1 February 1949 bound for Port Victoria, Australia, to load grain for the U.K., where she arrived in October after what has been described as the very last of the grain races around the Horn to Britain.

To briefly round out the ship's history, the *Pamir* was then put up for sale by her Finnish owners and was subsequently sold after having served as a grain hulk. This was in March 1951. Then, a group of German ship owners bought back the *Pamir*, thus rescuing her from the Belgian shipbreakers. Their idea was to convert the ship into a cargo-carrying training ship – which they did – and which had been the subject of so much consideration by the New Zealand government before they finally gave her up. Large sums of money were expended on the ship's conversion and the *Pamir* came out of refit late in 1951 as an auxiliary sailing ship. After a troubled first voyage, the ship came back to lie bankrupt in a European port. The ship was an economic disaster and required heavy subsidizing. However, the *Pamir* survived to eke out a precarious existence sailing between Germany and the east coast of South America, carrying cargo and cadets. Her tragic loss in this service was recorded in September 1957 when she was overwhelmed in a hurricane, with all but six of her 86-member crew going down with her.

When the *Pamir* had to be returned to Finland by the New Zealand government, many in that country were sad to see her go. When the news of her tragic loss was received, many people both in New Zealand and in Canada, and indeed elsewhere around the world, had to pause and reflect – a great ship was gone forever.

MEN WHO SAILED IN THE *PAMIR*

It is evident that without exception, the New Zealand men who served on this big ship cherish those days as high points in their careers. It had been an experience, a rare chance to go to sea in sail, and they are all keen to talk about it, even today. It is therefore fortunate for those of us on the Canadian west coast who are interested, to hear first-hand some of the personal and shipboard experiences when the *Pamir* made her three memorable visits to Vancouver. It is also appropriate to report about some of the men who served on this ship and what they ended up doing, for they themselves were examples of the value that many countries today place on training in sail. The word "Pamir" is almost like a password in New Zealand and almost everybody has some familiarity with the ship's history. There was and still is, great interest shown when conversation turns to the subject of the *Pamir*, and there seems to be a noticeable pride when the New Zealander refers to his country's association with the ship. The voyages of the *Pamir*, received tremendous publicity in New Zealand.

After the *Pamir*'s seizure in 1941 there followed a period of eight months during which the ship underwent survey, repairs and refit until, by the end of February the following year, she was classed +100A1 at Lloyd's and sailed on her maiden voyage on 30 March 1942. The government had first to decide what trade to put her in. By November, the year of her seizure, the Union Steamship Company, at the request of the government, took on the responsibility of manning and operating the ship. Although hundreds of letters came in seeking a berth on her, there was difficulty getting experienced seamen. Mates and masters were available within the ranks of the company; however, by the middle of March, the ship had signed on her full complement, several more than the crew carried by its former Finnish owners. Her crew was a very young one. The average age of the deck boys and ordinary seamen was 17½ years and that of the carpenter, bosun, sailmaker and able seamen 25½ years; the mates were also young men.

When the *Pamir* came out of her refit, some £8,000 had been spent on her and charged to the War Expenses Account. Most of her standing rigging had been renewed and a complete set of sails had been provided, as well as spares. The original estimate for alterations and renewals had been set at £2,500, but as the work progressed it was, of course, found that there was a lot more work and material required than had been first anticipated. Crew accommodation was improved and additional WCs, showers and wash basins were installed in their quarters. By the end of January, the costs getting the ship ready for sea had already exceeded £6,000. And after the experience gained on the first voyage, there was an additional expenditure of some £4,000 authorized for further alterations to the crew's space. In the end, such preliminary expenses totalled over £20,000.

Some of the pay rates then in force are of interest. The first master was signed on at £70 per month. The union agreement between the Federated Seamen's Union and the Union Steamship Company resulted in an able seaman's pay being £24 per month which included a war risk bonus of £4:7:0 per month. With new agreements over the period of the ship's operation, these rates rose and contributed to the increasing operation expenses of the subsequent voyages.

Today, in New Zealand, ex-crew members and officers of the *Pamir* have done very well in their chosen careers, with many of the men having achieved key positions in the marine field. There is no doubt that training in sail, even today, has value, in that it builds character, develops leadership and above all, teaches men to react with firm decision and coolness in the face of sometimes great difficulty. The benefits of training under sail now accrue to both men and women in various countries, and here in British Columbia, groups of young men and women can sign on board sailing vessels which have, in recent years, been built and entered in the programmes of S.A.L.T.S. (Sail and Life Training Society).

The memories of those trans-Pacific voyages to both Vancouver and San Francisco were a mixture of various emotions, both serious and lighthearted. The Americans treated the crew like heroes. The ship's first visit to "'Frisco" was the subject of many articles, and a programme was broadcast from the deck of the *Pamir* by one of the local radio stations. The master's report after completion of this first passage to the west coast contained some interesting comments to indicate how the ship and crew had performed. The first comment of note was the mention of a serious breakdown in the refrigeration equipment which, although repaired at San Francisco, was to be a continuing problem on the ship, and it will be recalled that trouble was still being experienced with the compressors on the later Vancouver voyages. Experience gained on this first voyage had also shown that there was need to provide a spare cabin for use as a hospital. With a larger crew being carried, the accommodation amidships, which formerly allowed room for such service, was entirely taken up, and when a patient needed tending or isolation, it meant having to make temporary shuffles in the accommodation. Many alterations to cabins were made en route to better suit the occupants.

Regarding the accommodation, the master objected to the boys being separated from the seamen and he re-arranged the distribution of berths so that an equal number of boys and men were in each forecastle. This resulted in an improvement and better harmony between the two groups. The majority of the boys were keen to learn, and the second mate conducted weekly lessons in seamanship and related topics. The master also recommended that as vacancies for ordinary seamen arose on future voyages, they be filled from the ranks of the boys, and requested the Marine Department and the Seamen's Union to arrange accordingly. In a similar manner this could be applied to the promotion of ordinary seamen to able seamen regardless of sea service. This idea set the precedent for the future voyages, and those who stayed with the ship rose through the ranks in this way.

The master also reported the failings of the ship's mechanical equipment, which although having been tested at Wellington, did not perform well under continuous operation. A lot of time was lost through breakdown of the oil winches with which the *Pamir* was fitted, and the generating plant suffered many stoppages. The equipment was given an overhaul while in San Francisco and was put in satisfactory order for loading.

Finally, the master's report mentioned perhaps the most important man aboard – the cook, who was entirely unsuitable. He was therefore "sacked" immediately on arrival back in Wellington, as was also the chief steward. In conclusion, the Master reported that he was generally well satisfied with the way the crew had settled down to sailing-ship conditions and that they had performed their duties well, the exception being an altercation between one crew member and the first mate, which was logged, in the traditional manner.

And so, the Marine Department and other government branches in New Zealand, as well as the Union Steamship Company, received generally good news about their charge and its first passage.

The fifth voyage to San Francisco had some exciting and tense moments. Northbound when the ship was well to the northeast of Hawaii, a submarine was sighted. The ship's log reported the sighting at 24° 31′ N and 146° 47′ W and described it as a large submarine. Those aboard the *Pamir* assumed that the sub was either out of torpedoes or its commander had respect for the ship in sail. A steep sea was running which prevented surface action and gunnery by the sub. The stranger was about a mile away with her decks awash in the seas and it shadowed the *Pamir* for some time. The *Pamir* wore away under all sail and ran, the sub disappeared and nothing further happened. Two U.S. ships had been sunk in the region where the *Pamir* would have to pass and she had been cautioned to be on the lookout.

While in San Francisco that voyage, one of her crewmen, Ken Wells, only 21, rescued a boy from the cold waters of the harbour. They had heard the cries for help near one of the neighbouring piers, and Ken was in the water in a flash and brought the boy in, being helped ashore by a shipmate who had thrown a line. This was December of 1944 and Mr. Wells recalled how bitterly cold the water was. He subsequently received a medal from the American authorities for his brave effort and, prior to receiving this award, and unknown to Ken, there had been correspondence with the New Zealand government about it, as the Americans wanted to publicly recognize his action. The New Zealand government, however, had to instruct that the matter be censored for the time being due to wartime security. Publicity about the *Pamir*'s early war voyages was, in the opinion of the New Zealand government, not desirable. Anyway, Ken Wells eventually received his recognition.

On the return passage to New Zealand this voyage, the ship was caught in a bad blow. She was away to the southwest of Rarotonga where on 17 February 1945, with a falling barometer, she was shortening sail. The wind rose to Force 11 in a heavy sea. As conditions grew worse, the master, Captain A. R. Champion, ordered all hands aloft to return to the deck. Owing to the inexperience of the crew in such conditions he considered it unsafe for the hands to remain aloft any longer. Then the gale backed and blew at Force 12-plus in squalls. The sails that were still set were blowing out except those on the mizzen, and the sheets of these were let fly for the safety of the ship.

The master decided to heave to and while doing so the foresail blew away. The wind now blew steadily at Force 12. A topmast backstay carried away and the starboard liferaft disappeared over the side. During this short-lived and violent hurricane the ship lost 18 sails, including several that had been furled – they were just torn from their yards. But the ship and its crew came through it all and the memories of those hours remain. The expenses of a voyage were determined to a great degree by the weather encountered – as can be appreciated by the above description.

The *Pamir* went into drydock at Oakland in March and October 1943, her second and third voyages. She underwent repairs, replacements and painting, and the bill came to some $16,000 to maintain her classification with Lloyd's. On the next voyage, more repairs were carried out for a further $10,000 (the October docking). The ship was struck by a U.S. naval tug in December 1944 while she was at her berth but only very minor damage resulted. The tug had been moving a floating dock down the Oakland harbour.

The above further illustrates voyage expenses.

In New Zealand today, there is a *Pamir* crew association. Their object is to meet once in a while to reminisce about former days aboard the ship. There is also a Cape Horner's Association, having among its membership ex-*Pamir* men. At meetings of such associations, former sailors of the *Pamir* have some good times recalling some of their exploits: there was one time in 'Frisco at night when one of the boys made a remark that didn't go down too well, "I was a bit cheeky in those days . . . next thing there was a click of a knife opening. I was half-way back to the ship before my partner had time to turn around!"

"We worked four hours on and four off and at times we really had to work hard and when three whistles blew everyone turned to in a hurry. In spite of our inexperience, it didn't take long to learn the ropes (figuratively and literally!), and within three weeks we could clamber up the ratlines quickly and walk nonchalantly with no hand holds along the yards. Fresh-water rationing was another topic – from a locked pump. After the cook had taken his allowance, it worked out to about a quart per man, of which a pint went into the communal lime juice supply. At times, the issue went down to a pint per man. With a sudden shower in the tropics, the scuppers were quickly blocked and out came the soap and clothes as the men washed themselves and their clothing side by side."

Then there were those tropical evenings, with the masts and yards moving across a starlit sky.

The traditional shark's tail was fitted to the end of the bowsprit every voyage – a mascot for fair winds.

When you went barefoot for 40 or 50 days and more, socks hurt your feet when you came to putting them on.

At times when laying across the yards fisting in the sail, the footropes would swing almost above the level of your head and the oilskins would be flapping up your back unless you had them tied down to your body. There was talk of the time when, as a boy, you were first sent up to the royal yard arm and all you could do was hang on scared stiff. But soon you got used to it and before long you were sliding down a rope to the deck instead of clambering down the ratlines.

Then there was the time of the sail drill and the Royal display when the ship was in London – somebody let the halyard go and the jib came down over a bunch of the guys on the forecastle – it didn't look very smart! One of the jokers signed on as a boy, and after the ship had been a day at sea, he sent a cablegram back to his parents to tell them so. There was the master who married a Canadian girl, the master who had a suit for every kind of weather. Or how about the joker who saved up his daily tot of rum and would have a couple of bottles stashed away by the end of the voyage? And when arriving back in New Zealand with the pilot and customs aboard, there would be great socializing and consumption of rum while somebody would be heaving cartons of cigarettes and canned salmon over the side onto the tug. And on and on the yarns would go. There were plenty of stories to tell.

When the Marine Department in Wellington allowed me to peruse their files on the *Pamir*, I was surprised to see the number of private individuals that had written over the years from places far and near asking about the ship when it was in service under the New Zealand flag. Many had intended writing books about the ship.

Whatever the result may have been in those endeavours, the men who made history with the *Pamir* in so far as New Zealand was concerned, were living books in themselves and a proud lot because of it. No doubt their recollections and pertinent records will be preserved in a country that is very proud of its maritime heritage.

Organizations such as the New Zealand Ship and Marine Society, which has a keen membership, had this goal in mind. The Maritime Museum in one of the harbour board buildings at Wellington contains among other excellent exhibits, the ensigns that the *Pamir* flew and in addition, and of particular interest, a photo of the ship during that dramatic moment off Cape Flattery.

It was a privilege for me to talk to some of the *Pamir* men, and it satisfied a long-sought desire to learn more about those days when the *Pamir* was on our west coast, and it was gratifying to see how interested these men all seemed to be in that part of their past. Through their courtesy to me and that of the marine and other departments of the government of New Zealand, I have been able to complete this account and thus reveal a lot of the interesting events and stories that most of us here on the west coast never really knew. The sharing of the information with the reader, to my mind, dictates that I further introduce some of those men who made this account possible and update their careers with, in some cases, the unfortunate announcement of their having passed on.

Both masters, the Champion brothers were from a seafaring family. A. R. Champion went back to his duty as pilot with the Lyttleton Harbour Board in New Zealand when he left the *Pamir*, and subsequently retired in New Zealand and is presently active in his late 80s and patron of the New Zealand *Pamir* Association. D. C. Champion married and settled in Vancouver and has since passed away. Both mate Galloway and radio officer Healy had served with D. C. Champion on Union ships before the days of the *Pamir* in the New Zealand service.

In looking through the crew lists of all the voyages of the *Pamir* under the New Zealand flag, it is interesting to observe that certain names repeat in every voyage or nearly every voyage, and one sees how certain men rose through the ranks in accordance with the policy established by the master on the first Pacific voyage.

Andy S. Keyworth, popular aboard ship and ashore, was one such name. Mr. Keyworth joined the ship on the first voyage as an able seaman. On succeeding voyages he served as bosun's mate, bosun, and then third mate. He missed the fifth voyage to sit for his second mate's ticket. On the next three voyages, the Vancouver voyages, he was the second mate. Captain Keyworth became a master on one of the Union steamships plying the Tasman Sea to Australia and recently retired as senior master of that company's fleet. A. F. Jenkins, now retired, became Captain Jenkins and a senior pilot with the Wellington Harbour Board and later the Harbourmaster. The first voyage crew list showed a deck boy by the name of Jenkins. The second voyage he is shown as an ordinary seaman. On the third, fourth and fifth voyages he was an able seaman. He missed the first two Vancouver voyages but on the last Vancouver voyage he had returned to the ship as her third mate. He again served as the third mate for the U.K. voyage. Later he joined the pilotage authority at Wellington.

F. M. Renner was another who had started out on the second voyage as an able seaman. He advanced successively on following voyages through bosun's mate, bosun and then third mate. He was the third mate on the first two Vancouver voyages and became a great friend of the Moodie family while the ship visited Vancouver. It was third mate Renner who had so much to do with the success of the ship's newspaper. He passed away several years ago.

G. S. Gunn, the boy who fell overboard on the second Vancouver voyage, started his service on the *Pamir* as deck boy on the first Vancouver voyage and on the following voyage rose to ordinary seaman. The last Vancouver voyage saw him as an able seaman, as did the succeeding Australian voyage. He sat for his third mate's ticket and served in that capacity on the U.K. voyage but had to leave the ship at Antwerp due to illness. Captain Gunn became the Harbourmaster, Port of Napier, New Zealand, and recently retired.

A. Cappiello, "Capy" to his mates, who ended up in Nelson, New Zealand with the Harbour Board there, was an able seaman on the first two Vancouver voyages and also signed on as able seaman for the very last voyage, when the *Pamir* was taken back to the U.K. under the Finnish flag after the ship had been handed over to her former owners.

J. MacDiarmid became bosun on the New Zealand Railways ferry *Aramoana* operating across Cook Strait between Wellington, and Picton on the South Island.

He had signed on the *Pamir* as a deck boy on the last San Francisco voyage and also made the next trip, to Vancouver.

P. Hunt, who became a skipper on a ship that regularly ran to the Chatham Islands off New Zealand South Island, had joined the *Pamir* on the fifth voyage to San Francisco as deck boy and also for the first Vancouver voyage. Next trip he was an ordinary seaman, and on the U.K. voyage he was an able seaman. He passed away several years ago while still at sea.

G. R. Inkster became Captain Inkster and Harbourmaster, Port of Nelson, New Zealand. He was an able seaman on the first Vancouver voyage and has contributed one of the photographs in this book. After returning to sea from his position as harbourmaster, he recently retired.

K. H. Wells, the boy who made the rescue in San Francisco harbour, became Captain Wells and skipper of a new tug belonging to the Nelson Harbour Board, after having been skipper for several years on the well-known and last of the little trading scows, the *Te Aroha*, which operated between Nelson, Wellington and the Sounds at the north end of South Island. He too has recently retired.

The list could go on and on, but one final example of a deepwaterman was D. W. (Bill) Galloway who became the respected Harbourmaster and Port Captain at Wellington, New Zealand. Bill had come to the *Pamir* on her fourth Pacific voyage under Captain A. R. Champion who had been appointed the master for that voyage. Bill had his second mate's ticket, and for the last San Francisco voyage he continued as second mate. He missed the next Pacific voyage to sit for his mate's ticket and subsequently joined the *Pamir* for the remaining Vancouver voyages in the capacity of first mate, as well as for the succeeding Australian voyage. Still only in his mid-twenties, Galloway left the ship on its return to Wellington to join the pilotage of that port's harbour board and went on to become the harbourmaster. As a young man, Bill Galloway joined the Erikson ship *Penang* in 1938 and as a matter of interest had tried to join the *Pamir* at that time. Life on the Erikson ships as a deck boy was not as easy as later to be experienced by young New Zealanders serving on the *Pamir*. Bill could remember a lot of his time being spent below, chipping and painting, chipping and painting! But he took it all in his stride and soon learned the ropes and his way about a ship. The *Penang* sailed from Port Victoria for England with grain and on the way to Cape Horn was dismasted. The ship limped into Port Chalmers (Dunedin, South Island) and effected repairs. It was a long passage before the ship reached England. Galloway ended up at Goteborg, Sweden, because the ship could not go into the Baltic on account of ice. They were laid up for four months. Then Russia attacked Finland. The ship sailed out into the Atlantic when the war broke out. They made a long haul down around the Cape to Mauritius and thence to New Zealand. When Bill Galloway arrived home it was a case of either going to war or staying at sea, so he went on steamers and later found himself serving in Egypt on a hospital ship. When he came back to New Zealand once more, a berth on the *Pamir* was available and so he was able to realize his first desire, that of shipping out on the *Pamir*.

But his first ship, the *Penang*, he fondly referred to as a beautiful little ship, and he had good memories of his time aboard her. Most of the crew were Swedish-Finns and he learned a lot of the Swedish language during that period. The *Penang* was later sunk by a German torpedo. Captain Galloway, the young man who went over the stern of the *Pamir* to rescue seaman Gunn, is well known in New Zealand, for he figured prominently in the *Wahine* disaster of 1968 in Wellington Harbour. The *Wahine* was an inter-island ferry that was overwhelmed in a hurricane as she entered the narrow confines of Wellington's magnificent harbour entrance. Many lives were lost in this tragic event, and Galloway was the man to succeed in boarding the stricken ship to help her master and assist in the rescue operations. Both he and the *Wahine*'s captain jumped overboard just before the ship capsized and after all the remaining passengers had been rescued.

Captain Galloway had a tremendous collection of photos and material concerning his days on the *Penang* and also to a lesser extent, the *Pamir*. He had fond memories of his days in sail and he gave freely of his time to talk about it and to show his pictures.

In parting, he said, on my thanking him so much for his time and information, "Well, we get out of life what we put into it!" I think he learned that a long time ago, perhaps when on the *Penang*.

It is with great sadness to hear that Bill Galloway, after retiring from a most successful career only a few years ago, was killed in an automobile accident.

PART TWO

THE TOWBOATS INVOLVED WITH THE BARQUE *PAMIR*

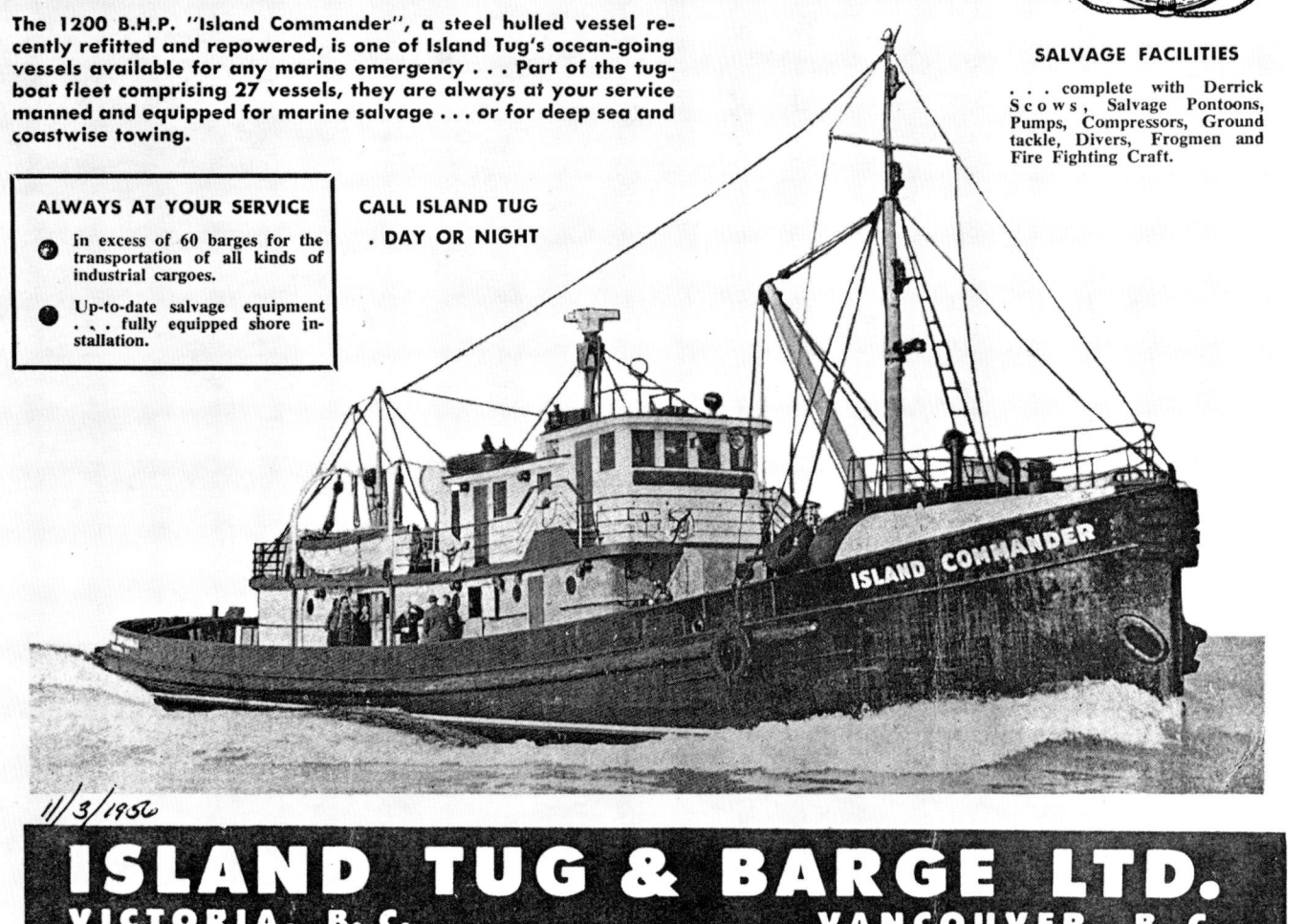

Marine Salvage
Deep Sea and Coastwise Towing

The 1200 B.H.P. "Island Commander", a steel hulled vessel recently refitted and repowered, is one of Island Tug's ocean-going vessels available for any marine emergency . . . Part of the tugboat fleet comprising 27 vessels, they are always at your service manned and equipped for marine salvage . . . or for deep sea and coastwise towing.

ALWAYS AT YOUR SERVICE
- In excess of 60 barges for the transportation of all kinds of industrial cargoes.
- Up-to-date salvage equipment . . . fully equipped shore installation.

CALL ISLAND TUG
. DAY OR NIGHT

SALVAGE FACILITIES
. . . complete with Derrick Scows, Salvage Pontoons, Pumps, Compressors, Ground tackle, Divers, Frogmen and Fire Fighting Craft.

ISLAND TUG & BARGE LTD.
VICTORIA, B.C.   VANCOUVER, B.C.

ISLAND TUG AND BARGE LIMITED

This company was one of the principal towing firms on the British Columbia coast. It had been founded in 1925 by H. B. Elworthy who had been with the B.C. Salvage Company, the first salvage company in British Columbia at the turn of the century.

The company first concentrated their operations on service to the forest industry as their fleet grew. After a decade, the fleet had grown to 11 tugs, 40 scows and 7 barges. It had been a period when the local towboating industry was converting to diesel tugs. There were also many experienced coastal mariners available to enlist in the expanding company.

In the 1930s several laid-up sailing ships were acquired and fitted out for hog fuel (chips and sawdust) barge service to transport this commodity from Canadian sawmills to U.S. pulp mills. The subsequent acquisition of tugs like the *Island Commander*, *Island Warrior* and *Snohomish* was suitable to this service, whose routes were in part on open ocean.

The purchase of the ex-U.S. Coast Guard cutter *Snohomish* in fact launched the company into the deep-sea towing and salvage business, and this vessel became the company's flagship during the 1940s.

The company pioneered the era of large, self-dumping log barges which needed the large and powerful tugs it then had for towing them. In the early 1950s former oil tankers were acquired and converted for this purpose and as well, additional powerful tugs were acquired. Several U.S. Maritime Commission surplus tugs were purchased after the war, so that by the late 1940s the company fleet had grown to include 15 tugs, many scows and 10 barges (included in the fleet at this time were the three oil-burning steam tugs, *Snohomish*, *Island Warrior* and *Burrard Chief*). The further acquisition of the vessels *Sudbury* and *Sudbury II* in the 1950s gained the company fame as the principal salvage company in the Pacific. High seas operations had become routine – operations no longer being confined to the coast. Some epic tows and salvage assignments were completed during this period. By 1961, some 30 ships had been towed across the Pacific by company tugs.

The towboat industry on the British Columbia coast underwent a process of development which saw the formation of many one-boat operations grow into multiple-vessel fleets – Island Tug and Barge Limited being typical. And, there were many mergers and takeovers through the years as the industry progressed to its present state.

Island Tug and Barge Limited had always been associated with the family name Elworthy. When Mr. Elworthy left Island Tug in 1942 to form Straits Towing at Vancouver, it was only a couple of years before he was back as owner of the company along with McKeen of Straits Towing and Foss of the well-known Puget Sound Towing Company. But in 1946, these principals separated, with Mr. Elworthy taking over complete control of Island Tug, and this is when the company underwent major changes, in that their fleet was increased and modernized and equipped to handle the increasing log transport business.

There were further acquisitions by the company: in 1952 they took over the towing firm, Young and Gore of Vancouver, and in 1959, the Victoria Tug Company. By the end of the 1950s, Island Tug was one of a handful of major towing companies on the coast that were involved in major re-organizations and mergers which, by 1970, had seen the emergence of two giant towing corporations dominating the industry.

Their operations had expanded to include covered barge service to isolated communities on Vancouver Island on a regular schedule (the *Island Commander* was often used in this service) and rail and tanker barge services.

In 1960, the company was sold to McAllister Towing Limited of Montreal, which itself was jointly owned by McAllister Brothers Inc. of New York and Sogemines Limited of Montreal. Mr. Elworthy was retained under a management agreement. Great competition had developed after legislation ended the towboat companies' agreement to charge common rates for their services. As such, the larger companies manoeuvred to maintain their position in the industry.

The development of the large, ocean-going barge to handle a variety of commodities saw the launching of two large bulk carriers in 1962 and a couple years later, the first of the large, self-dumping and self-loading log barges were launched.

There were then about 30 tugs and over 100 scows and barges in the operations of the newly-organized company.

In 1970, Seaspan International was formed, which came about through a deal worked out between Dillingham Corporation of Honolulu, which, the previous year, had acquired all of the shares of the Vancouver Tug Company, and Genstar (formerly Sogemines), to merge the two firms, Vancouver Tug and Island Tug, calling the combined operation Van. Isle Tug and Barge, subsequently to be Seaspan International Ltd.

The new organization then owned 65 tugs and more than 250 scows and barges. The name Elworthy was still among the board of directors. This company, along with Rivtow Straits, became the dominant organizations of the British Columbia towing industry.

There was continued expansion between the two despite internal management problems, and in 1972, Seaspan bought Yorke and Son, a pioneer in the railcar barge service on the coast. The following year, a merger with Crowly Maritime of San Francisco and Federal Commerce and Navigation of Montreal resulted in the establishment of the Arctic Transportation Company. Further international ventures were undertaken in the North Sea, Saudi Arabia, and the Mediterranean, and in 1977 Gulf of Georgia towing sold out to Seaspan.

The now multinational Seaspan dominates the British Columbia towboat industry and as can be seen, it had its beginnings with Island Tug and Barge Limited back in 1925.

Halibut Steamer
in the Gulf of Alaska,
circa 1914-16.

THE HALIBUT STEAMERS

Before chronicling the career of the *Island Commander* and *Island Warrior*, it is appropriate to review the development of the halibut fishing industry on the Pacific coast, because, as originally built, they were an important part of it.

Although the halibut had long been fished by the Indians (particularly the Makahs at Cape Flattery) for their own sustenance, and then by small vessels providing fresh fish to local settlements, it was not until the late 1880s that commercial fishing for this species commenced with the arrival of sailing schooners from the east coast, where fishing knowhow for the Atlantic species of halibut had been acquired by New England interests over a period of years. Knowledge brought back east about the Pacific species coupled with a diminishing fishery on the Atlantic, induced these entrepreneurs to make the long haul out to the Pacific coast. They commenced fishing off Cape Flattery and unloaded their catches at Tacoma, on Puget Sound, the terminus of the new Northern Pacific Railroad, for shipment to eastern markets.

It was soon evident that powered vessels would be most suitable for this fishery, both for navigational ability in often confined waters, and for speed and dependability in handling a product that had to be landed at trans-shipping ports as soon as possible. The era of the sailing fishing schooner was consequently very short lived.

Thus, the era of the halibut steamers (generally acknowledged as from 1890 to 1920) began. At first, vessels used were types converted from other services, but in 1898, a new vessel was brought out, having been designed and launched specifically for this trade and appropriately named *New England*, for it was these eastern interests in the U.S. markets that dominated this new industry in the Pacific region.

The New England Fishing Company (NEFCO) had started operations at Vancouver, British Columbia, in 1894 (the new Canadian Pacific Railroad offered a better service for the American boat catches by coupling refrigerator cars to their fast continental trains, a practice that was not allowed on the U.S. train routes). Additional steamers were chartered or acquired for this company's operations, and the fishing extended along the coast and offshore regions to the north. These steamers all used dories and "set-line" gear.

A small British (Canadian) fleet had also entered this fishery.

By 1907, a new British company had been formed, the Canadian Fish and Cold Storage Company Limited, whose objectives were to build a fish cold storage plant at Prince Rupert, British Columbia, to service the growing steamer fleets and provide trans-shipping facilities and acquire their own vessels to enter the fishery. The man to be in charge of the development of this new operation was the former manager of the NEFCO operation at Vancouver.

There were several smaller companies entering the industry: some one-vessel outfits, some successful, and others falling into bankruptcy. Consequently, there were failures, mergers, and takeovers in this new industry with resultant migration of experienced and key personnel.

Another company, the Canadian Fishing Company (CANFISCO) had been formed by Vancouver entrepreneurs in 1906, operating three steamers, but by 1909 they were bought out by the NEFCO organization and accordingly became a subsidiary of that company. The Canadian Fishing Company had a subsidiary, the Atlin Fishing Company at Prince Rupert which was later, in 1912, bought by NEFCO, and so the parent American firm then had a presence in the new halibut centre of Prince Rupert.

In 1910, the Atlin Construction Company was incorporated to "carry out the business of contracting and construction in all its branches." This was the construction organization of the previously incorporated Canadian Fish and Cold Storage Company Limited. The new cold storage plant was completed at Seal Cove and became operational in the summer of 1912. It was referred to as the "Hull" since company officials were originally from Hull, England, as were some of the steamer captains. The first halibut frozen at the plant was in April 1912 (this plant was demolished in 1984).

The company had three vessels built that year (1912) in England for their expanding Pacific operation. When these three steamers arrived at Prince Rupert, the port's halibut landings increased dramatically in 1913. The three vessels were named: *Andrew Kelly*, *James Carruthers* and *George E. Foster*, all after principals of the company. When built, they were fitted out for otter trawling but as this method of fishing the Pacific halibut proved to be inefficient, upon their arrival at Prince Rupert they were immediately converted for dory fishing and, eventually, longlining. These vessels were used in the initial exploitation of the fishery west of Cape Spencer in the Gulf of Alaska, off the Alaskan panhandle. Soon after these vessels' entry into the industry, the *James Carruthers* introduced longlining after the British practice using the "liners" out of the well-known Lancashire fishing port of Fleetwood on the Irish Sea. This method proved successful and involved less crew, with the ability to fish in inclement weather (often the case in the Gulf of Alaska) with less danger and easier work than the dory method. All three of the new vessels converted to longlining directly from the ship, and the stern chute was introduced for greater safety in setting out the gear. And so, the fishing method that has long prevailed in the industry originated with this first experimental use.

Landings at Prince Rupert increased, especially in 1915 when U.S. vessels were permitted to unload their catches there. During 1917-19, the *George E. Foster* and the *James Carruthers* used the otter trawl method for obtaining other species due to wartime demand and an available government subsidy.

The completion of the transcontinental railroads in both Canada and the United States, and the construction of fish cold storage plants, provided the means for fast and reliable freight service for a perishable commodity, and halibut became the first, fresh, frozen-fish species to be shipped in carload lots to the east. The first shipment out of Prince Rupert by the Canadian Fish and Cold Storage Company Limited was made on 30 September 1914, the Grand Trunk Pacific Railroad having become operational the previous year. Prince Rupert became known as the "halibut capital."

When the three new steel vessels were brought out from England, they were registered in the ownership of the Atlin Construction Company, Prince Rupert, but with Port of Registry at Grimsby, England. In 1916, this company was absorbed into the Canadian Fish and Cold Storage Company Limited. A new ownership under this latter name was registered for the vessels in Lloyd's Register for 1918-19.

By 1915, the unrestricted fishing of the previous 25 years was seen to have taken its toll on the fish stocks. From then on, especially after the First World War, when demand for the product also declined, the industry was severely curtailed, and by the mid-1920s the International Halibut Commission, established in 1923, after much negotiation between Canada and the U.S., had introduced conservation programmes and closed seasons which restricted the catches.

This period saw the rise and decline of the company-owned steamers in the halibut fishery with their eventual replacement by the smaller private vessel – the powered halibut schooner. The companies found it more economical to buy from the independent vessels.

By the mid-1920s, conversion to longlining was universal and by 1932, dory fishing was only being carried out by a couple of vessels.

Prior to 1923, there were no restrictions on this fishery – there was only the 3-mile limit along the coastline and the operation was entirely dictated by markets, profit, and the will to expend effort with the dangers involved. But after the signing of the 1923 Convention, and succeeding conventions of later years, this industry became the most regulated fishery in the world. No other nations were involved until the late 1950s, after which, in spite of International Pacific Halibut Commission (IPHC) monitoring and regulations after the 1923 Convention, the stocks once again were seen to be dwindling, due in great measure to foreign fishing pressure.

The adoption of the 200-mile offshore limit in the late 1970s was the latest measure to preserve the interests of the U.S. and Canada in this important fishery.

In the 1920s, vessels like the *Andrew Kelly* and the *George E. Foster* could no longer operate economically within the industry and so they were laid up at Prince Rupert. These vessels remained on registry until the 1930s, still with home port listed as Grimsby. In 1932, their home port registry was changed to Prince Rupert.

Both of these vessels had been built at Selby in North Yorkshire, and were described on register as ketch-rigged, steam fishing trawlers. Selby is about 35 miles upstream from Hull on the River Ouse, a tributary of the Humber River. Cochrane and Sons Limited, the builders, originating from Scotland, became renowned as the foremost builders of steam trawlers in Britain. Their vessels were regarded as the "Rolls Royces" of trawlers (this company is still in business today at the same location producing all types of small vessels, tugs and support vessels to industry).

The vessels were fitted out and engined at Hull by C D. Holmes and Company Limited, Engineers and Boilermakers, a company long established in the designing and building of propulsion machinery, boilers, auxiliaries, propellers and trawl winches. The vessels, after being launched sideways at Selby, were towed down the channel to Hull for their fitting out. Grimsby, where the trawlers were first registered, is 15 miles downstream from Hull at the entrance to the North Sea – the two harbours noted as the largest fishing ports in Britain.

The *Andrew Kelly* was listed in 1936 as having changed her ownership to Dominion Tug and Barge Company Limited, still with registry at Prince Rupert. The company eventually took the machinery out of her and installed it in another tug, so the *Kelly* became laid up once more, finally at North Vancouver.

The *George E. Foster* also changed ownership, in 1934, when she was sold to the Westward Towing Company Limited, eventually to be registered at Vancouver. She was acquired by the Dominion Tug and Barge Company along with the *Kelly* in 1936, and subsequently given an extensive conversion. She again changed ownership in 1938 to the San Juan Towing Company Limited, Vancouver, and remained in this ownership until 1941.

And so, some of the first vessels of the halibut fishery were thus converted to tow boats. They had been poorly looked after during their lay-up after the end of their fishing service and their machinery needed a complete overhaul. Conversion of these steam trawlers to tugs presented difficulties since their machinery, boilers, and such, were all in the after half of the vessel, which left little room to install towing winches on the after decks.

On both the *Kelly* and the *Foster*, the large trawl winch on the foredeck was initially used as a tow winch, running the towline under the wheelhouse and over and through the machinery spaces, including a fairlead through the stack. The original design of these double-drum winches was for a forward pull, with trawl warps used in side trawling leading forward through sheaves at the foremast and then out through the gallows and to the net connections. As towboats, the strain was directly aft and so in heavy going with large tows, the tug skippers watched this towing arrangement closely and sometimes dogged these winches with anchoring lines forward.

The acquisition of such steam trawlers was the first use of steel tugs in the British Columbia towing industry.

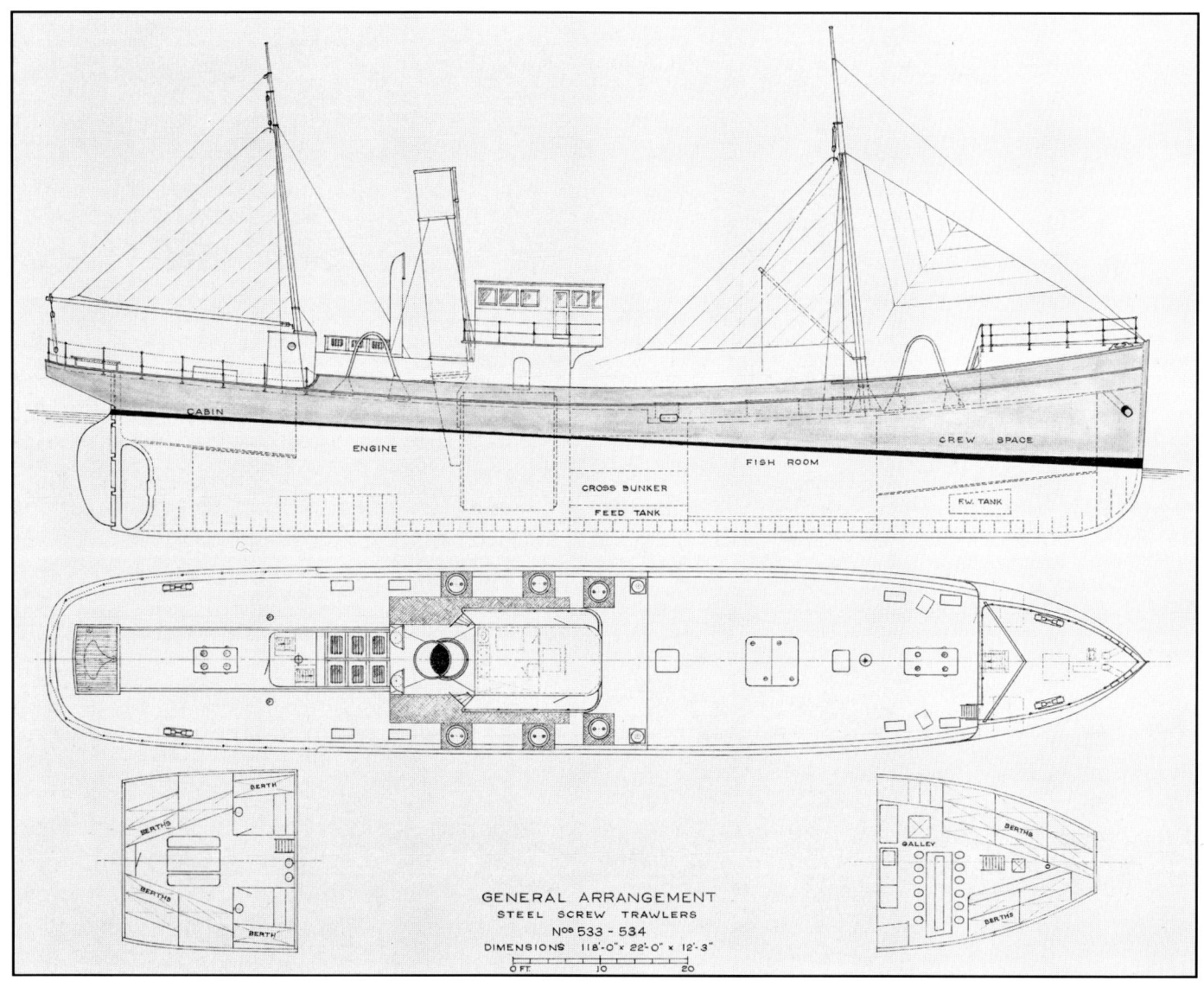

Andrew Kelly Hull No. 534 and *George E. Foster* Hull No. 533.
Plan redrawn by the author from the builder's General Arrangement Plan provided by Cochrane Shipbuilders Ltd., Selby, Yorkshire.

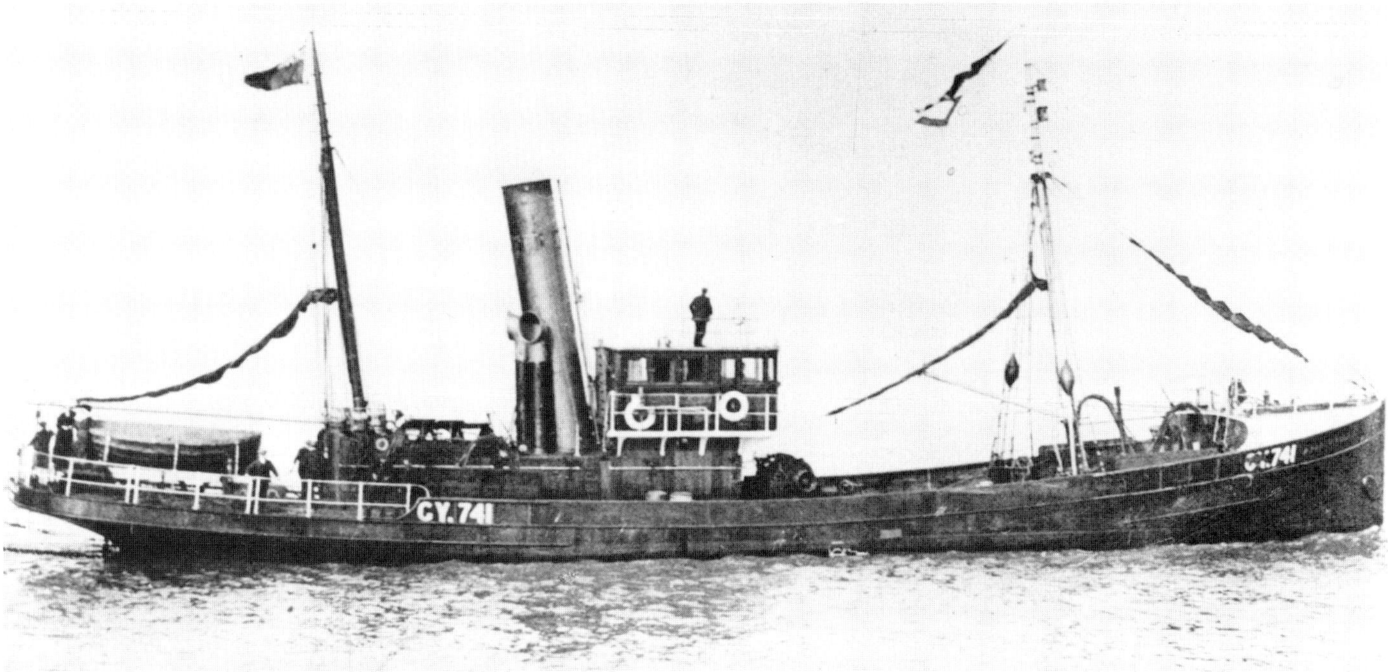

GET

Andrew Kelly, as commissioned, 1913.

VMM

VMM

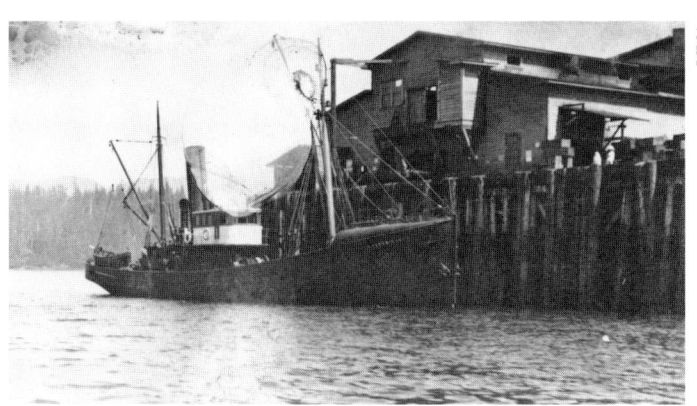

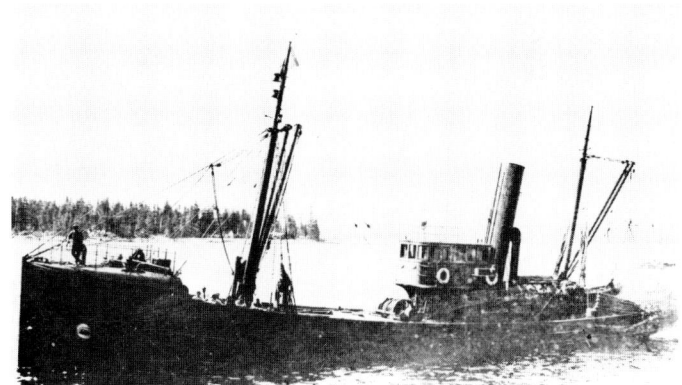

circa 1913-17

Andrew Kelley halibut fishing in the Gulf of Alaska 1913-17.

circa 1920

The fishing fleet at Prince Rupert, 1913. *George E. Foster*, fourth from left.

Scenes on board 1913-17

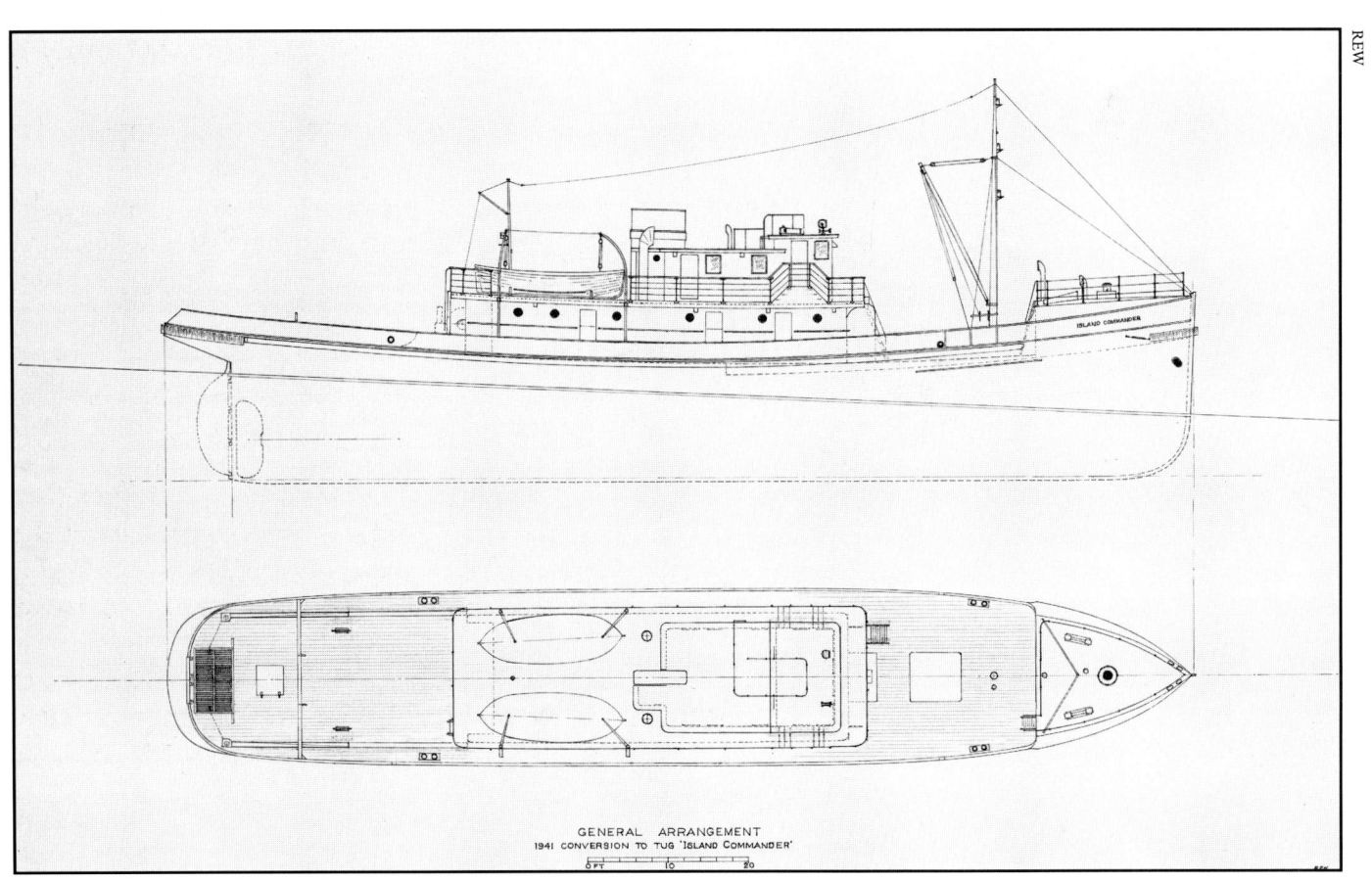

Island Commander General Arrangement Plan, 1941 conversion.

ISLAND COMMANDER

After her change of ownership and use as a tug, the *Andrew Kelly*, in 1938, ceased to be listed with Lloyd's, and she was laid up and not converted as her sister ship was.

But in 1941, Island Tug and Barge Limited of Victoria, British Columbia, after inspecting her hull, decided to purchase her. The vessel was completely rebuilt and a 500-hp. diesel engine installed by the North Vancouver Ship Repair Company Limited. Her former trawler appearance was thus greatly changed from that of her sister ship. The vessel was renamed *Island Commander* in 1942 and registered at Vancouver.

The McIntosh-Seymour engine installed in her was obtained from the wrecked twin-screw motor ship, *Boobyalla*. It was of the blast injection type with a huge air compressor – a slow-turning, quiet-running and easy-to-handle engine, but later was converted to solid injection to give better service. At first, the towing winch installed was operated by a separate truck engine, which proved unsatisfactory.

The vessel was first chartered to the U.S. government for service in the Alaska-Aleutian area with the U.S. Army Transport Service (ATS). In 1944, when she was returned to Victoria, she was used in heavier towing service along the British Columbia coast, often towing the hog fuel barges (converted sailing ship hulls) between Port Alberni and the Washington State pulp mills, and, as related herein, was involved with the *Pamir* tows on three occasions.

She made some memorable ocean tows. On one trip, while towing a barge with several tugs on it from San Pedro for New Westminster, she threw a propeller blade off Eureka, California. The tug and her tow were towed into port by the U.S. Coast Guard and had to remain there for several days until the company (ITB) flagship *Snohomish* could steam down there to bring them north.

In the early 1950s she participated in the tow of the river boat *Delta Queen* from San Francisco to Kitimat, British Columbia, where that vessel was set up as a dormitory for construction workers at the new Alcan project there. At this time her registry had been changed to the Port of Victoria, British Columbia.

In 1956 she was rebuilt and repowered with a 1,200-hp. 8-cylinder Union diesel, direct reversing (Union Diesel Engine Company, Oakland, California). The Burrard Iron Works Limited, Vancouver, agents for the Union diesels, obtained the nearly new engine from Florida, stripped and completely overhauled it and delivered it to the Island Tug facilities at Victoria where the company's own personnel installed it. As well, new fuel and water tanks were added to give the vessel the capability of remaining at sea for at least 30 days. A new steel deck and towing winch were also installed, this towing winch still in use on the vessel although now hydraulically operated. The vessel's stack was altered giving a lower, more streamlined profile. This project resulted in yet another deep-sea tug available for long-distance towing and salvage work during a period of expansion by the company.

The vessel continued in the Island Tug fleet until the 1970s when the company was absorbed by Seaspan International. Seaspan declared her obsolete and sold her in November 1971 to Island Sea Marine Limited (K. Higgs).

In 1975-76 the vessel was again repowered, at Seattle, with a 1,750-hp. 16-cylinder EMD GM 567 BC diesel engine and at the same time a steel dodger was constructed around the wheelhouse deck. In 1978, a new wheelhouse and skipper's cabin were built on in aluminum, thus giving the vessel a major change of appearance, the wheelhouse then extending across the entire deck width thus eliminating the walk around former side decks. Access to the larger wheelhouse was via aft port and starboard doors as well as from down below. Interior berthing arrangements were also revised by the new owner. The gas-powered engine driving the towing winch (built by ITB in their major 1956 conversion) was eliminated in 1976 when the winch operation was converted to hydraulic operation. In 1983, the former gas-engine-driven anchor windlass was converted to hydraulic operation.

The *Island Commander* has served the British Columbia towing industry for 50 years – she has been referred to as the last of the Grimsby trawlers and her turtle-back forecastle, characteristic of the North Sea trawlers, still sets her apart from the rest of the towing fleets' vessels on the B.C. coast.

There has recently been a proposal to repatriate the vessel to Grimsby as a heritage vessel for display there. Whether this becomes reality remains to be seen.

Meanwhile, the *Island Commander* is still serving the British Columbia towing industry.

The vessel's first master during her northern service in the Aleutians with the ATS was Captain Jack Gillam. He was also the skipper on the first *Pamir* tow. The very first trip after conversion to a diesel tug was skippered by the well-known Rollie Robertson. The well-known and -liked skipper, "Drydie" Jones (Evan Drysdale Jones) took over the vessel from Captain Gillam in the 1940s. Drydie, who had commenced his seafaring life as a teenager on the famous old tug *Lorne* in the 1920s, soon acquired his master's ticket. He became mate on the *Lorne* by the late 1920s. Drydie Jones just recently (1989) passed away at Victoria and is missed by all his towboating acquaintances. Captain Charlie Goodwin commanded the vessel both before and after her 1956 refit and conversion and he was followed by Captain George Hovel. Captain G. W. (Joe) Higgs skippered the vessel for twelve years when she was on the barge run around the north end of Vancouver Island as well as towing log barges from various ports on the coast.

Ken Higgs, her present skipper and owner, takes a keen interest in his vessel's special significance as the last of the trawler tugs.

Lloyd's Register 1945-46

Island Commander – steel tug
Official number 134745. Built 1912 by Cochrane and Sons, Selby, England
Signal letters VCZG

Registered dimensions: length 118.0 feet, l.o.a. 128 feet, Breadth 22.0 feet, Depth 11.5 feet, Gross tonnage 271

Port of Registry: Vancouver, British Columbia

Owner: Island Tug and Barge Limited

Engine: Diesel 6 cyl. 16" – 24" stroke
500 hp. 149 nhp. (Society Rule)

Engine maker: McIntosh and Seymour, Auburn, New York.

Alaska with ATS wartime grey and after gun turret, 1942.

Barkley Sound, August 1946.

Victoria Harbour, 1949.

After major refit and re-powering, 1956.

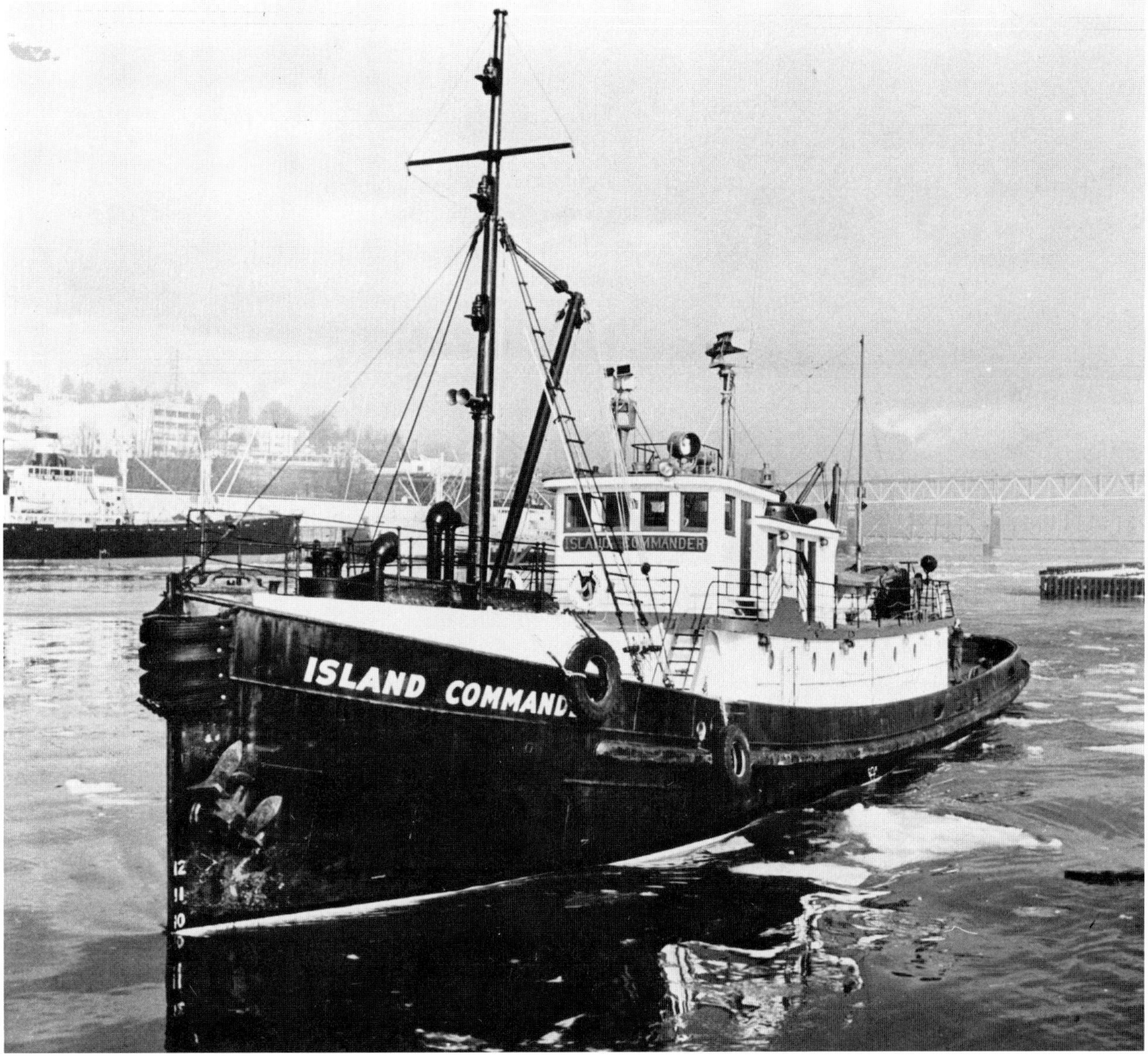

VMM

New Westminster, davits removed, 1962.

New wheel house.

Vancouver, steel dodger around wheel house, 1977.

1980-90.

ISLAND WARRIOR

In her 1938 change of ownership, the *George B. Foster* was reconditioned throughout, being fitted for fuel oil with new tanks and steel decks in conformation with the new requirements of the Dominion Steamboat Regulations. New steam winches for towing were installed, and also a radio telephone, all in readiness to fit the tug for service on the west coast of Vancouver Island.

Island Tug and Barge Limited of Victoria, British Columbia, purchased the *George E. Foster* in 1941. They retained her steam engine and equipment and renamed her *Island Warrior*, registered at Vancouver, and employed her on both inside and outside coastal waters in general towing services, and she was particularly useful in towing large-section log booms. The vessel's availability for the last of the *Pamir* tows was perhaps significant in that both the tug and the vessel towed were representatives of the last of an era: the *Pamir* being the last of the large commercial carriers of the sailing ship era, and the *Island Warrior* being one of the last remaining steam vessels being used in towboating on the British Columbia coast. Consideration was given to re-engining her with a diesel in 1956 (as with her sister ship, *Island Commander*) but her owners sold her in 1958 and she was scrapped. Island Tug and Barge Limited replaced her with a new, modern, 90-foot diesel tug with 1,500 hp. while retaining the same name.

The first master of the converted and re-fitted *George B. Foster* in 1938 was Captain Frank Unwin. The skipper of the vessel at the time of the second pick-up of the *Pamir* off Cape Flattery was Captain Charlie Goodwin, a veteran towboat skipper on the coast, and then employed with Island Tug. And, as has been related, he was commended for his performance with the tug in picking up the sailing ship under very difficult conditions. The final tow of the *Pamir* from Union Bay, Vancouver Island, was also under the command of Captain Goodwin. The name Goodwin was well known on the British Columbia coast, being a seafaring family with their own towing company, started by their father and subsequently operated by Charlie and his brothers, all of who became tug-boat masters. Charlie passed away many years ago and was remembered as one of the popular skippers in the Island Tug fleet.

Other skippers of the *Island Warrior* were Jim Talbott, George Dance and Bob Ryder, her last one.

Lloyd's Register 1945-46

Island Warrior – steel tug
Official number 134744. Built 1912 by Cochrane and Sons, Selby, England
Signal letters VGQL

Registered dimensions: Length 118.0 feet, l.o.a. 128 feet, Breadth 22.0 feet, Depth 11.5 feet, Gross tonnage 243

Port of Registry: Vancouver, British Columbia

Owner: Island Tug and Barge Limited

Engine: Triple expansion steam – 3-cyl. 12" × 21" × 34" – 24" stroke
58 rhp. (power by ships' registry)
500 hp. (indicated horsepower)

Engine maker: C. D. Holmes and Company Limited, Hull, England.

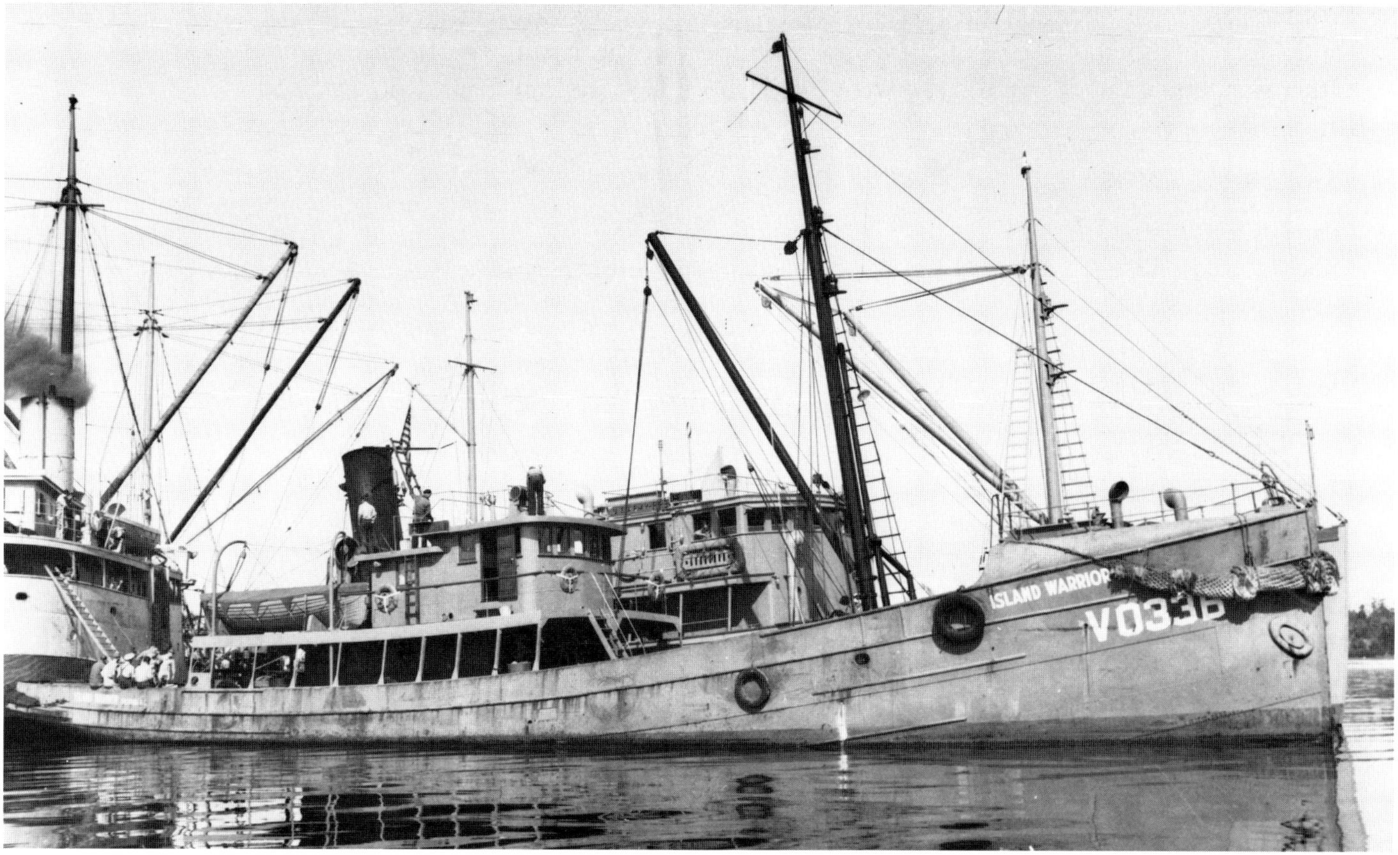

PSMHS No.1330

Wartime grey and ID No., 1942.

PMRV

1944

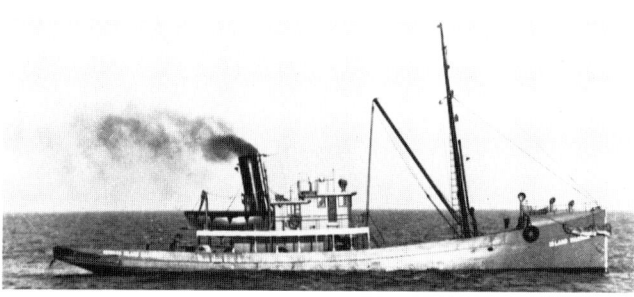

1950s

1946

Being scrapped, 1958.

SNOHOMISH

This vessel was launched as cutter No. 16 in March 1908 as a result of a modernization programme approved by the U.S. Congress in 1897. Along with two sister ships, she entered service with the U.S. Revenue Cutter Service and was sent out to the Pacific coast where she took up station at Neah Bay, Washington, in May 1909 and later was stationed at Port Angeles, Washington. In 1915 she became a U.S. Coast Guard cutter when both the Lifesaving Service and the Revenue Cutter Service came under the Coast Guard. In 1917 the vessel entered naval service after the U.S. had entered the First World War. She steamed back to the east coast and served in Atlantic wartime towing duties. Upon the conclusion of hostilities, she returned to the Pacific coast to resume her patrol and rescue duties. She served in Alaska on the Bering Sea patrols, and intermittently at Astoria, Oregon, but for the greater part of her career she was based at Port Angeles. She was decommissioned in 1934.

During her career as a Revenue and then Coast Guard cutter, she achieved fame because of her many rescue missions to shipwrecks on both the Washington and Canadian coasts and saved many lives.

As originally built, the vessel had an open forecastle deck and carried armament on bridge wings either side of the wheelhouse. A departure from the original 1908 General Arrangement Plan was the extension of the boat deck out to the extreme side in way of the boat stations for easier and safer handling of the boats. The open arrangement of her foredeck was found unsatisfactory in heavy weather and a major reconstruction plan was carried out as shown on the 1915 General Arrangement Plan revision. Thus, her outboard profile was markedly changed, with her forecastle deck being closed in and this deck extended right aft to her main mast and outboard to her sides. She retained this reconstruction appearance until her last days although through the years, modifications, such as a three-inch gun mounted on the foredeck, a radio shack built on the after deck between the stack and the engine-room skylight, and a flying bridge enclosure, were added.

The vessel was purchased by the Puget Sound Tug and Barge Company of Seattle after her decommissioning, and a couple of years later, in 1937, she was bought by the Island Tug and Barge Limited of Victoria, British Columbia, who fitted her out to serve as the company's principal towing vessel. In her Island Tug days, she had a flying bridge with wings supported on stanchions to her main or wheelhouse deck – a modification carried out soon after her acquisition. The vessel was still a coal burner and had no towing winch when she came into the Island Tug fleet. A self-spooling towing machine was installed with a drum capacity of 2,000 feet of two-inch cable and later she was converted to an oil burner. Her navigation equipment was brought up to modern standards with a radio direction finder and radio telephone being installed. The vessel was then well equipped for her intended service in ocean towing and salvage.

The *Snohomish* survived a sinking in 1941 when her tow rammed her. After this she served in Alaska during the war years, along with other vessels of the Island Tug fleet with the U.S. Army Transport Service. In 1944 she resumed her major towing services with the company, both coastal and deep sea. In fact, it was the acquisition of the *Snohomish* that launched the company into deep-sea towing and salvage service. The vessel remained with the Island Tug fleet until 1947 when she departed Seattle in an epic tow, for the time, with six U.S. Army diesel tugs secured aboard one of the company's log barges that had been modified for this particular tow. The destination was Buenos Aires, Argentina – a 10,000-mile tow.

Upon arrival there, the vessel changed ownership. She was sold to the Argentine navy which at the time had been expanding its auxiliary fleet with the acquisition of many ex-U.S. Army tugs. She was renamed *Mataras* and thereafter served under the Argentine flag. She was operated there in salvage and towing work, but was soon put up for sale again and was finally sold by auction in August 1960 to a towing firm in Buenos Aires. She was rebuilt in 1962 and renamed *Ona Sol* and continued in towing service. In 1971 further improvements were made to her towing machine and her combustion system. Her power was listed as 1,600 hp., still steam-engined. But in 1980, her over 30 years of service under the Argentine flag ended when the vessel was finally sold for scrap to local dealers at the Port of Buenos Aires.

When the *Snohomish* came under Canadian ownership and registry, she was placed under the command of Captain Fred MacFarlane, a veteran towboat master who had recently joined Island Tug. Captain MacFarlane remained the vessel's master throughout her Canadian ownership, including the *Pamir* tow, and finally the long tow to Argentina. After the sale of the *Snohomish*, he took command of other principal towing vessels of the Canadian company before going ashore to become the shore captain for the company until his retirement. When Captain MacFarlane passed away in 1965, he was described as one of British Columbia's most colourful master mariners.

The mate of the *Snohomish* during the *Pamir* tow was Jim Talbott. Many years later he vividly recalled those anxious moments just before the *Pamir* slipped her towline in the gale off Cape Flattery. Mr. Talbott became a deep-sea towing master and was involved in some memorable tows across the North Pacific from Japan when the Alaska pipeline was being constructed. Mr. Talbott passed away in 1983 but is remembered fondly by those who served with him on several of the Island Tug vessels. Captain George Dance, now retired, started his towboating career on the *Snohomish* and became her mate, as did captains Korra Larsen and Ron Newell. Walter Smith and Cece Fletcher were chief engineers in the vessel's early years with the company.

Gone are the days of steam towboating on the coast, but the *Snohomish*, with her U.S. Coast Guard heritage will always be remembered. Anyone who served on her will recall the sounds and smells of her steam power with the rhythm and relative silence that could only be experienced on a steam vessel. Her big destroyer wheel guided her from 56° North in the Aleutians to 56° South off Cape Horn during her distinguished career.

She was, in the 1940s, a powerful acquisition to the British Columbia towing fleet.

Lloyd's Register 1945-46

Snohomish – steel tug
Official number 158954. Built 1908 by Pusey and Jones Company, Wilmington, Delaware, U.S.A.
Signal letters VCPJ

Registered dimensions: Length 139.6 feet, l.o.a. 152 feet, Breadth 29.3 feet, Depth 15.1 feet, Gross Tonnage 549

Port of Registry: Victoria, British Columbia

Owner: Island Tug and Barge Limited

Engine: Triple-expansion steam – 3-cyl. 18" × 29" × 47" – 30" stroke 123 nhp. – 11-ft., four-bladed propeller, maximum speed 14 knots 1,250 hp. (indicated horsepower)

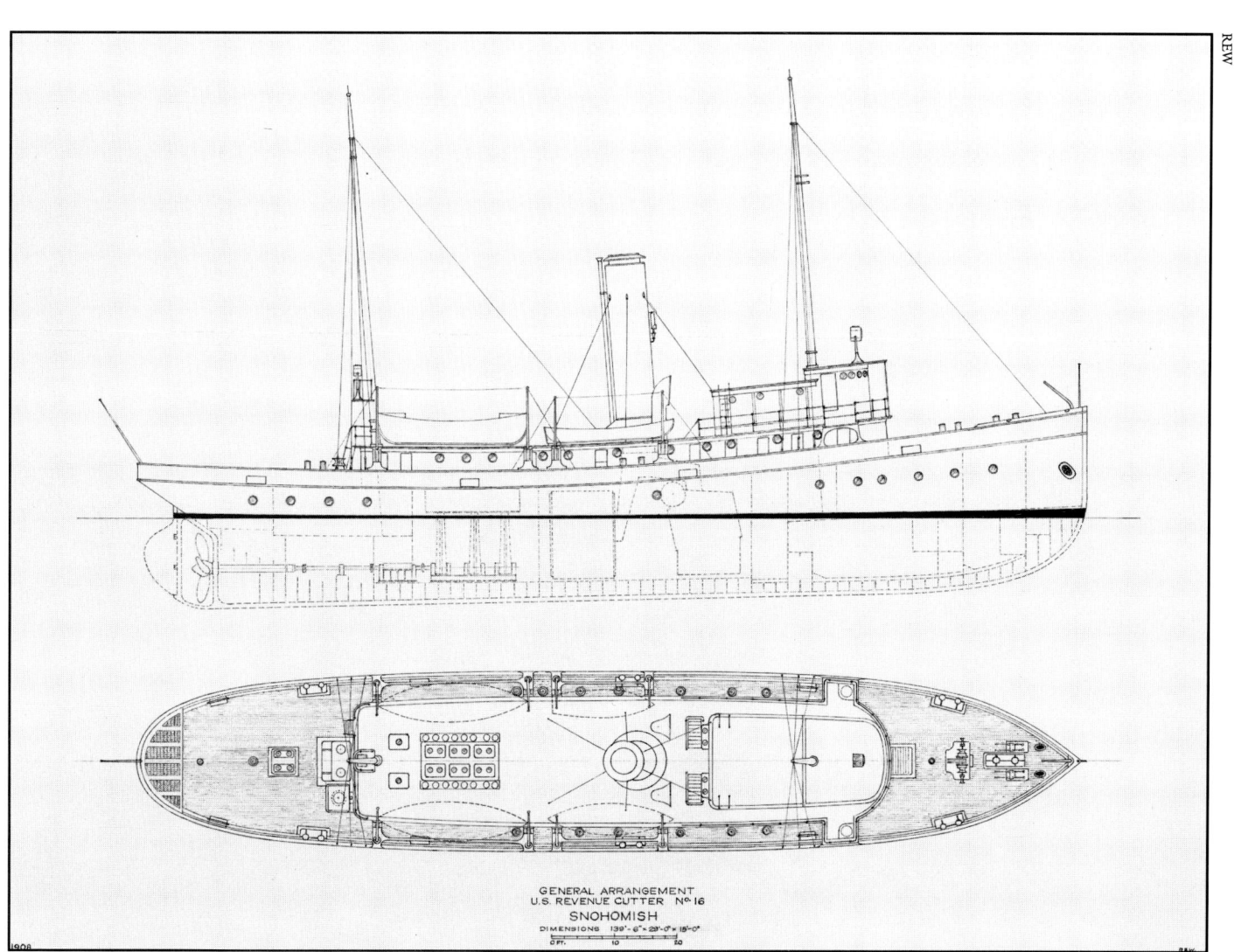

Snohomish General Arrangement Plan, USRC No. 16, 1908.
Plan redrawn by the author from builder's plans provided by the National Archives, Washington, D.C.

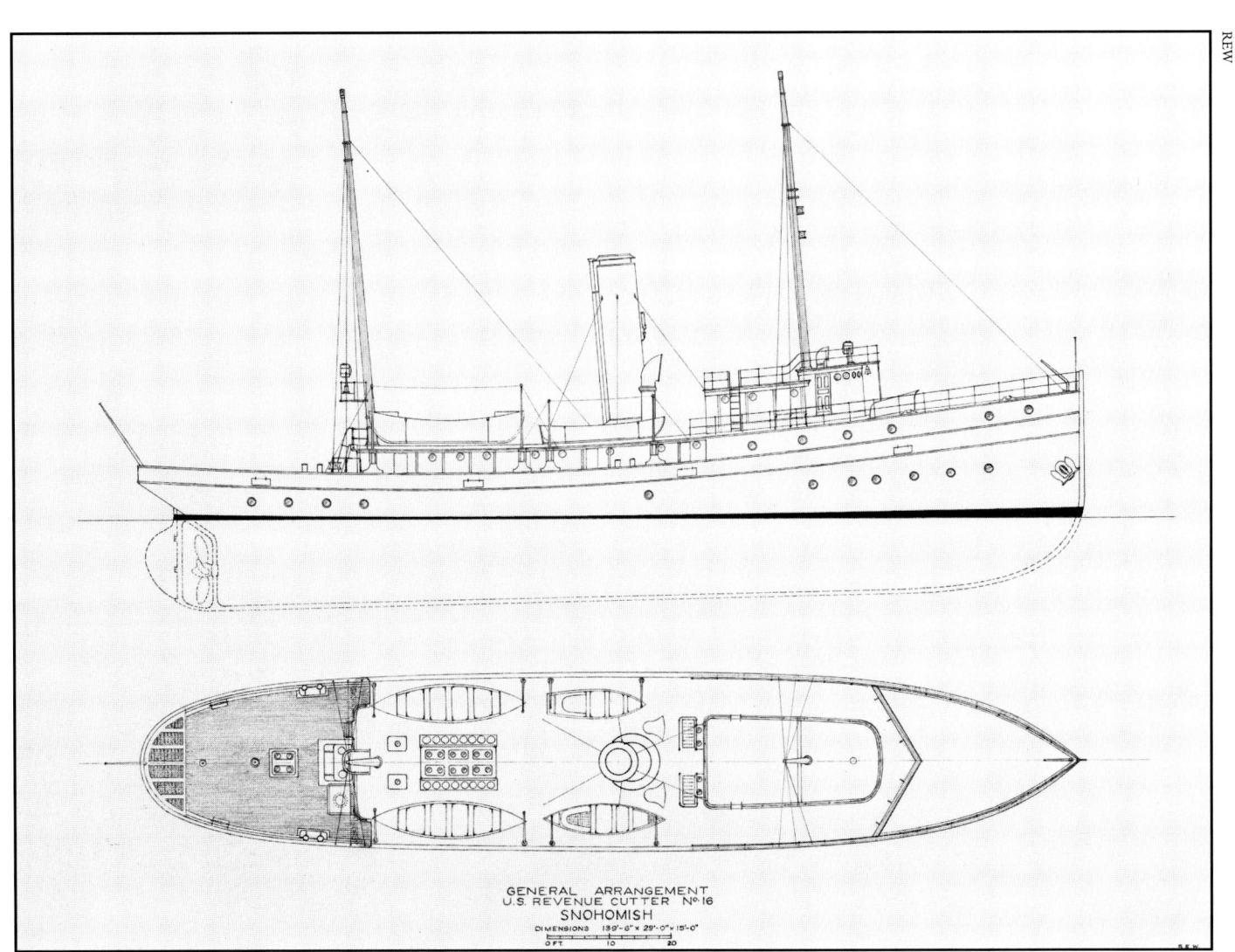

Snohomish General Arrangement Plan, USRC No. 16, 1915.
Plan redrawn by the author from builder's plans provided by the National Archives, Washington, D.C.

Seattle, April 1909, just after her arrival.

Port Angeles, 1912.

As reconstructed, Seattle, *circa* 1917.

On dock, 1922.

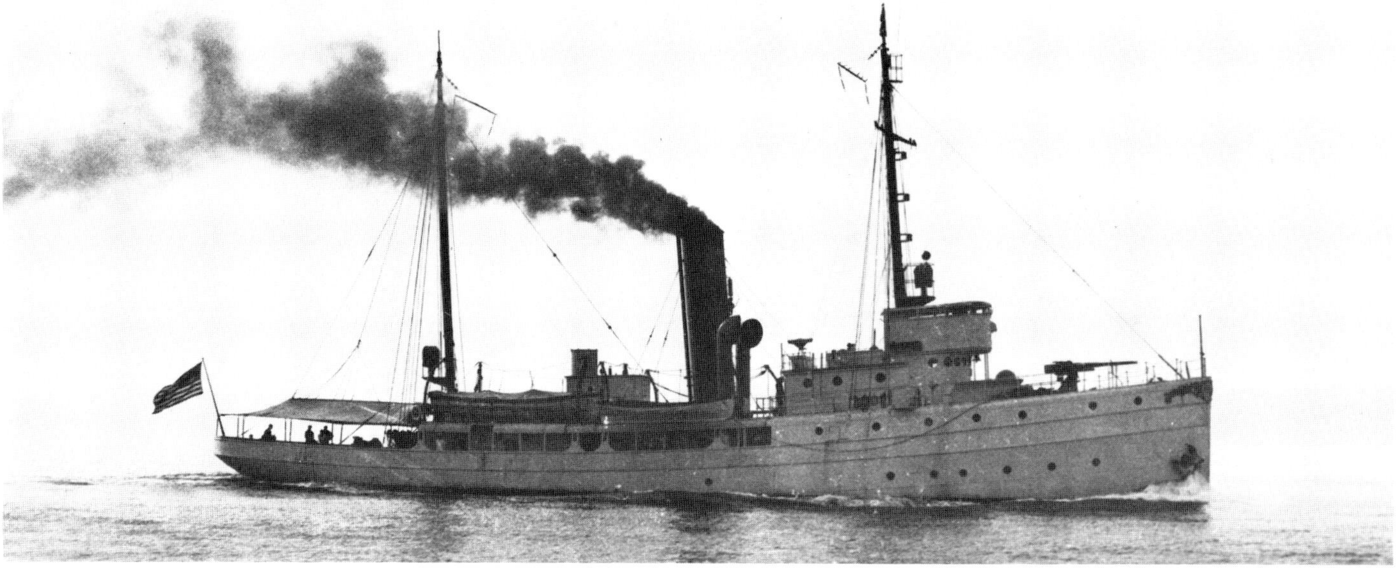

PSMHS No.2368

Bering Sea Patrol, 1920s.

CGMNW

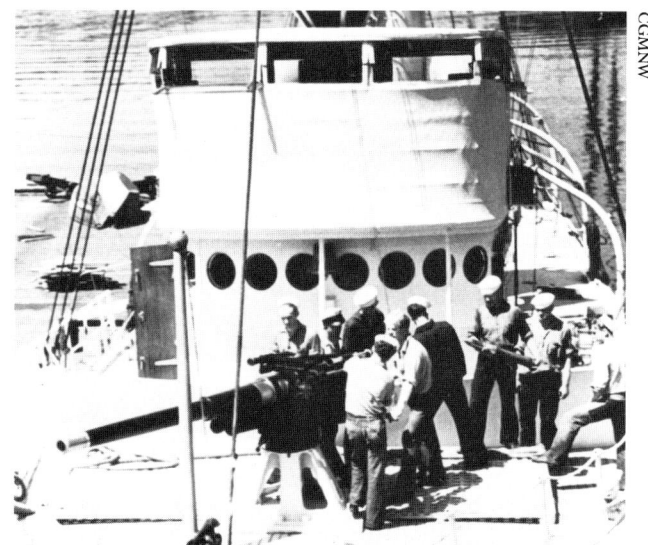

Flybridge enclosure
and 3″ gun, 1920s.

Puget Sound Tug and Barge, 1937.

Island Tug and Barge Ltd., 1939.

Wartime grey, flybridge wing and gun turret added for service with ATS.

MMBC

After wartime service, 1944.

The epic tow for Buenos Aires, 1947.

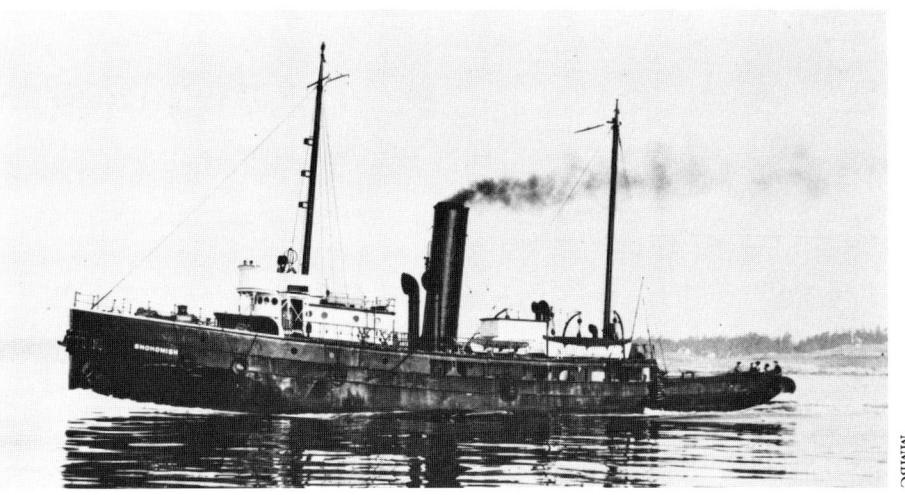

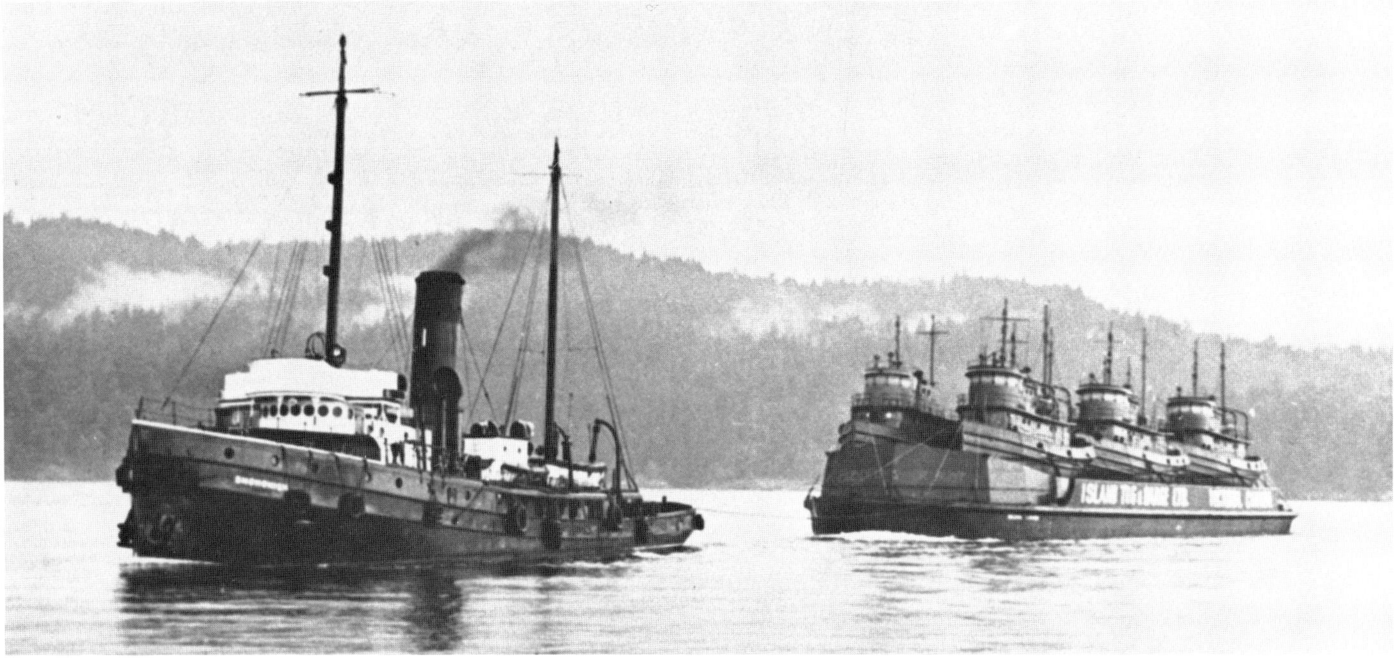

MMBC

ROBERT PRESTON

This vessel was originally built for Preston-Mann Towing Company Limited for the log-towing trade, being one of the larger wooden-hulled tugs on the coast at the time. (Of the early towboats on the coast during the first couple of decades of the century, one of the larger fleets assembled belonged to an engineer named Preston and a captain named Mann – they had five tugs and later built the *Robert Preston*. Their company became known as Preston-Mann and by 1942 there were ten tugs in this fleet.)

During 1942, this fleet was acquired by H. Elworthy of Island Tug and Barge Limited, Victoria, and McKeen of Standard Towing Company of Vancouver, and the new firm, Straits Towing and Salvage Company Limited, was formed. Such buy-outs and mergers of the various towboat companies on the coast continued for the next thirty years until finally, almost all of them were consolidated under two large corporations.

The *Robert Preston*, therefore, became a Straits Towing Company vessel. She was chartered to the U.S. Army Transport Service and was employed in towing barges from Seattle to Alaska, and served in the Aleutians. She returned to the British Columbia coast in 1944 and was a participant in the *Pamir* tows in 1945 and 1946. In 1949, the company renamed her *Johnstone Strait*.

The vessel was sold to the Dola Towing Company (1954) Limited of Vancouver in 1954, was re-registered at Vancouver and given the new name, *Prestige II*. She was used in the railway barge service for the CPR to Vancouver Island and the British Columbia Railway to Squamish, and, after that rail line extended through to North Vancouver, she went into service with Island Tug and Barge Limited between Squamish, North Vancouver, Victoria and Seattle in rail barge service.

In 1959 the company changed her name to *Prestige*. In 1969, she lay out of service at Vancouver. At that time she and the *Master* (now restored and operated at Vancouver as a heritage vessel) were the only surviving steam tugs on the British Columbia coast.

The vessel was sold, as she could not compete with the newer steel towing vessels of greater power and requiring less crew that were being built under government subsidies.

In 1970 she was purchased by Martin Higgs, her former skipper, and Ken Turner, and transferred to Gibsons for renovation and return to active towing, but after a couple of years she was sold again, to American owners. After this she never towed again and was used as a live-aboard.

In 1983 she was lying at Bellingham, Washington, again up for sale and declared a public eyesore and ordered removed. She was purchased by another Washington owner who had the vessel towed to Blaine where it was intended to restore her. Neglect, vandalism, and rot had taken their toll and she had to be pumped daily to keep afloat. Finally, this grand old steam tug sank at her anchor in Drayton Harbour in October 1988.

She sat on the mud, her wheelhouse top and foremast just protruding above the surface – a sad sight and end for a fine vessel.

When the *Robert Preston* was taken north during the early war years in the U.S. Army service, she was under the command of Captain Ellice Cavin, who later, after the vessel's return to Island Tug, became the well-known master of the *Island Champion* and was remembered for his guidance of the famous swim of the Juan de Fuca Strait by Marilyn Bell.

During the *Pamir* tows, her master was Captain Steve Fairhurst, and Wayne Lusk, now Captain Lusk, retired, was a deckhand. In 1944 her long-time chief engineer, Adam Baker, passed away.

Lloyd's Register 1945-46

Robert Preston – wood tug
Official number 150873. Built 1923 by Westminster Marine Railway Company Limited, B.C.
Signal letters VGLJ

Registered dimensions: Length 99.8 feet, Breadth 24.0 feet, Depth 14.1 feet, Gross tonnage 236

Port of Registry: New Westminster

Owner: Straits Towing and Salvage Company, Ltd.

Engine: Triple-expansion steam – 3-cyl. 11" × 20" × 32" – 24" stroke
51 rhp. (power by ship's registry)
500 bhp.
7'6" four-bladed propeller

Engine maker: McKie and Baxter, Glasgow, Scotland

AS

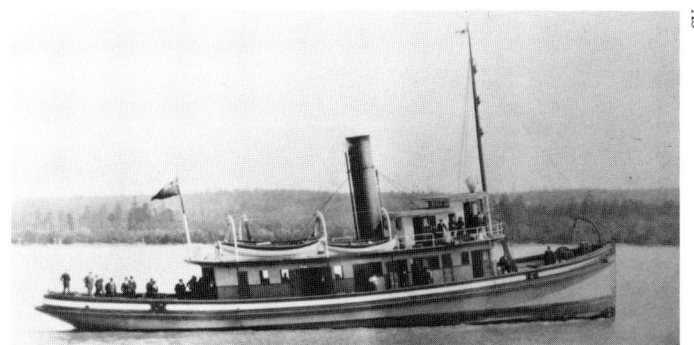

Commissioning and trials, 1923.

FC

circa 1930s

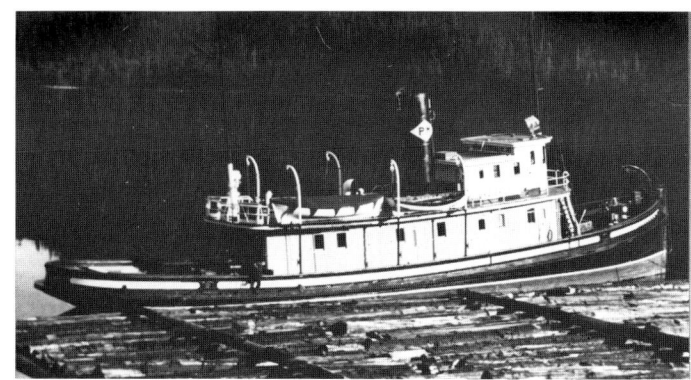

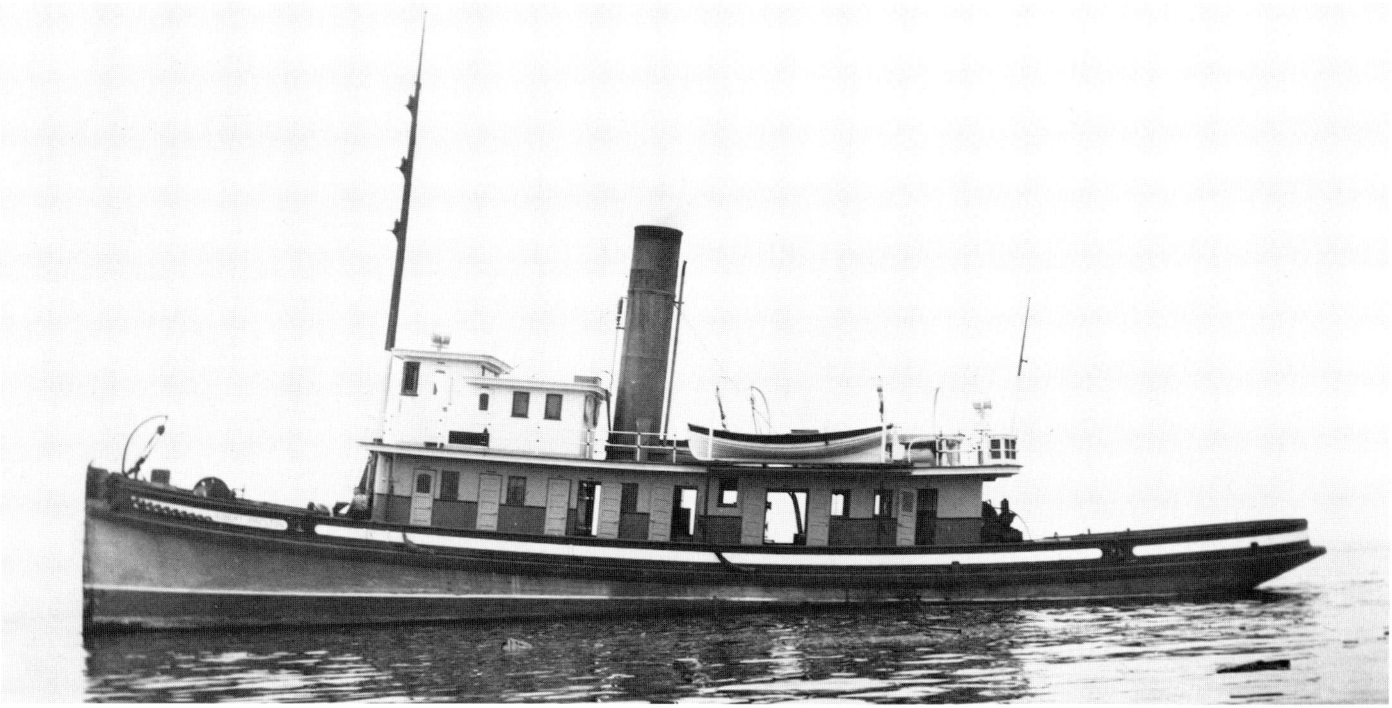

VMM

circa 1920s

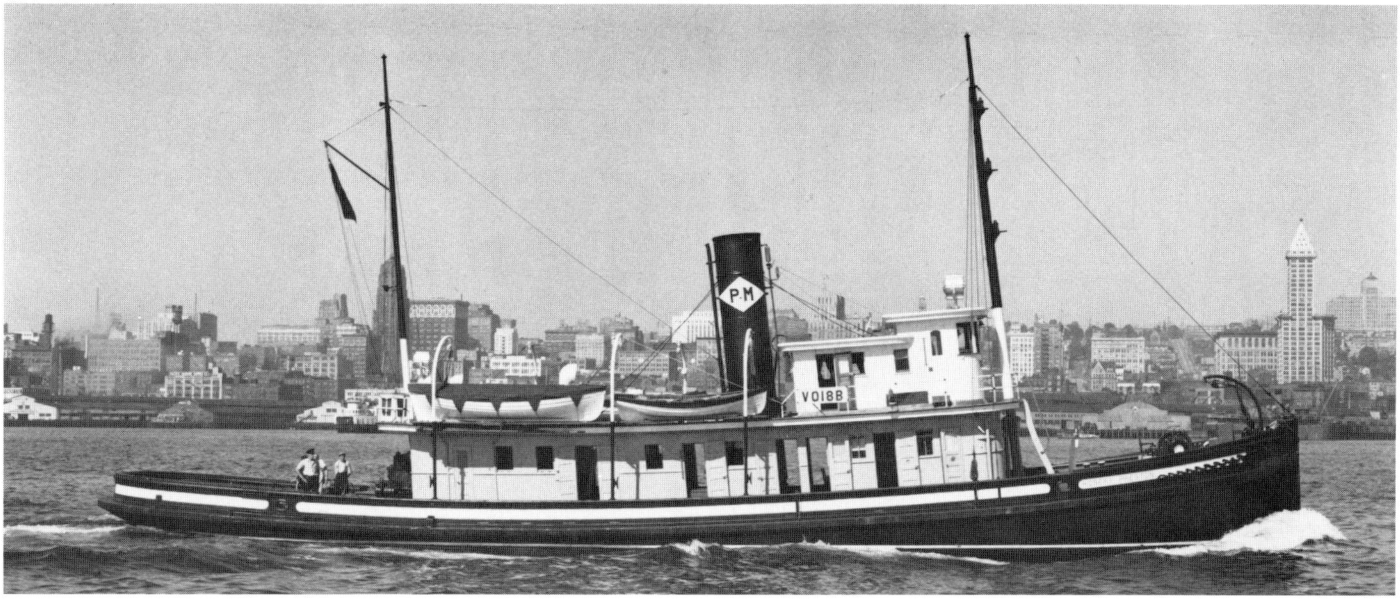

PSMHS No.736

Seattle, 1940.

FC

On after deck.

ASLPCA 134-243

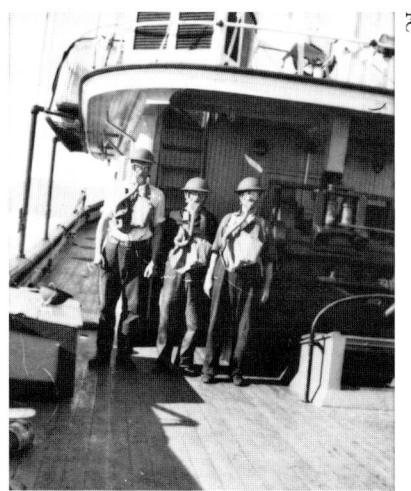

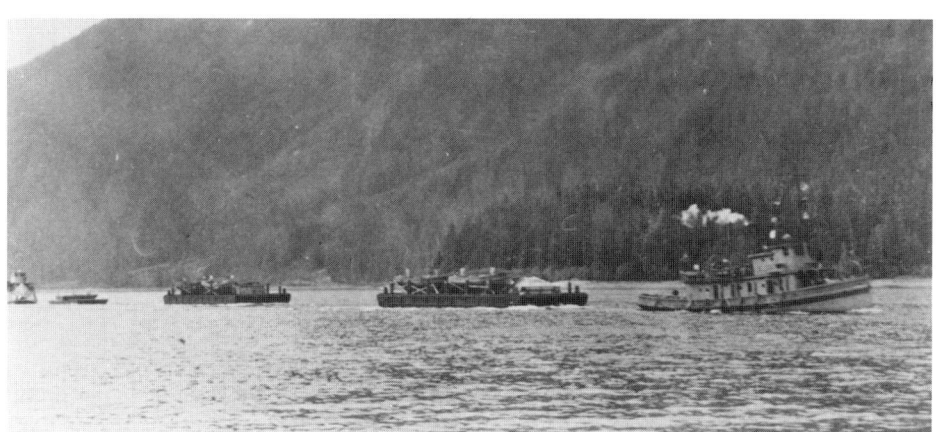

Alaska, 1943, with ATS.

Vancouver (Dola), 1955, as *Prestige II*.

Blaine, Washington, 1988, as *Prestige*.

APPENDIX

THE BARQUE *PAMIR*

The ship was launched in 1905 by Blohm and Voss, Hamburg, for ship owner Ferdinand Laeisz. He had pioneered the Chilean nitrate trade and built up a fleet of superb and fast steel ships that became known as the flying "P" Line – all his vessels being named beginning with the letter "P."

To endure the rigours of the trade around Cape Horn these sailing ships were strongly built and well found in every respect and the *Pamir*, being one of the last built, represented perfection in the design of such sailing ships.

A full bridge deck amidships was a characteristic of these new vessels which housed the officers and crew, thus replacing accommodations in forecastle and poop sections of older vessels. Catwalks connected this bridge deck with the forecastle and poop decks – all these features in the interest of greater crew comfort and safety.

The ship steered with a double wheel located abaft the charthouse on the bridge deck. This wheel was connected by heavy wires running over fairleads to the rudder quadrant. The rudder was a semi-balanced design.

Some particulars of the *Pamir* in her New Zealand service were:

Registered dimensions:

Length 316 feet, breadth 46 feet, depth 27 feet

Gross tonnage 2,796, New tonnage: 2,522, Forecastle 38 feet, Bridge deck 66 feet, Poop deck 29 feet

Cargo and ballast capacity: approximately 4,500 tons on a loaded draft of 23 feet 4¾ inches

Signal letters assigned: ZMKQ

Total sail area: 37,000 square feet

Forward fresh water capacity: 4,200 gallons
Aft fresh water capacity: 5,900 gallons

Displacement at 23 feet 5½ inches: 6,565 tons

Freeboard at full load displacement: 5 feet 8 inches

Fore, main and mizzen masts: 168 feet deck to truck
Jigger mast: 135 feet deck to truck

Lower yards: 92 feet, Lower topsail yards 85 feet, Upper topsail yards 80 feet, Lower topgallant yards 69 feet, Upper topgallant yards 62 feet, Royal yards 47 feet, Bowsprit 48 feet (external), Spanker boom 53 feet, Lower gaff 46 feet, Upper gaff 37 feet

All masts and spars of steel

Standing rigging: approximately 5,500 yards of steel wire set up for the most part with box screws.

Mechanical equipment: 4 15-hp. semi-diesel engines operating winches, one of which could be connected to the windlass for heaving the anchor and the capstan on the forecastle head.

A refrigeration plant installed in her New Zealand service gave constant trouble during the trans-Pacific voyages. Originally a diesel installation running the compressor via belt, the plant operation was changed to an electric-driven arrangement via the main generator.

In latter Pacific voyages, the main generator, a 7½kw. 110V DC, was driven by a 9-hp. Witte engine. This provided enough power to operate the radio, electric light within the ship, and the refrigeration plant.

An emergency (standby) generator, a 1kw. 110V DC, was driven by a Fairbanks-Morse 3-hp. kerosene engine.

Radio equipment consisted of a 250-watt transmitter, giving Morse on 600, 705 and 800 meters and radio telephone on 150 meters with two receivers, long and short wave.

VOYAGES OF THE BARQUE *PAMIR*
(dates and voyage times included where known)

UNDER GERMAN FLAG

Maiden Voyage

Depart Hamburg October 1905, arrive Valparaiso, 79 days
Depart Iquique (nitrates), arrive Hamburg 1906, 79 days

Depart Hamburg late 1906, arrive Valparaiso, 64 days
Depart Iquique (nitrates), arrive Hamburg 1907, 75 days

Similar voyages until 1914

Depart Hamburg early 1914, arrive Chile
Depart Taltal July 1914 (nitrates) (outbreak of war), arrive Tenerife October 1914
Laid up in neutral port
Depart Tenerife March 1920, arrive Hamburg April 1920
(discharge cargo loaded at Taltal in 1914)

Depart Hamburg under tow, arrive Naples July 1920
(in accordance with terms of Treaty of Versailles vessel surrendered to Italy)
Depart Naples October 1920 under tow, arrive Castellamare – laid up
Depart Castellamare under tow, arrive Genoa October 1922 – laid up
Depart Genoa February 1924 under tow, arrive Hamburg March 1924
Refit and return to German flag

Depart Hamburg March 1925, arrive Talcahuano May 1925, 74 days
Depart Chile (nitrates), arrive Hamburg

Depart Hamburg December 1925. Put into Falmouth for repairs
Arrive Chile

Vessel remained in Chilean trade 1926-1931

1929: outward passage 75 days, inward passage 86 days (Iquique to Bruges)

1931: arrive Hamburg July – laid up

1931: November – sold to Erikson, Mariehamn, Aland

UNDER FINNISH FLAG

Depart Hamburg (in ballast) 1932, arrive Port Lincoln, 87 days
Depart Wallaroo (wheat), arrive Falmouth, 103 days
Discharge at London

Vessel sailed to Mariehamn for refit

Depart Copenhagen (in ballast) 1932, arrive Port Lincoln Dec. 1932, 77 days
Depart Port Victoria (wheat), arrive Falmouth, 93 days
Discharge at Belfast

Depart Kotka (lumber) August 1933, arrive East London Nov. 1933, 97 days
Depart East London (in ballast), arrive Port Victoria Jan. 1934, 30 days
Depart Port Victoria, arrive Sydney, 13 days
Depart Sydney (wheat) March 1934, arrive Falmouth July 1934, 118 days
Discharge London

Depart Copenhagen (in ballast) 1935, arrive Port Lincoln, 77 days
Depart South Australia (wheat) 1935, arrive Falmouth 1935, 109 days
Discharge at Dublin

Depart Dublin (in ballast) October 1935, arrive Port Victoria Dec. 1935, 78 days
Depart South Australia (wheat) 1936, arrive Queenstown, 98 days
Discharge at Birkenhead

Vessel sailed to Mariehamn for refit and drydocking at Copenhagen

Depart Copenhagen (in ballast) 1936, arrive Port Lincoln 1936, 98 days
Depart Port Lincoln (wheat) Feb. 1937, arrive Falmouth May 1937, 98 days
Discharge at Hull

Depart Hull (in ballast) July 1937, arrive Seychelles Islands October 1937, 95 days
Depart Seychelles Islands, arrive Astov Island, 7 days
Loaded guano
Depart Astov Island (guano) Nov. 1937, arrive Auckland January 1938
Discharge and drydocked

Depart Auckland (in ballast) Feb. 1938, arrive Noumea, 11 days
Depart Noumea (nickel ore) April 1938, arrive Weser River July 1938, 106 days

Depart Nordenham August 1938, arrive Goteborg 1938, 12 days
Refit and drydocked

Depart Goteborg (in ballast) 1938, arrive Port Victoria 1938, 91 days
Depart South Australia (wheat) 1939, arrive Falmouth 1939, 96 days
Discharge at Southampton June 1939
Depart Southampton (in ballast) June 1939, arrive Goteborg – laid up

November 30, 1939 – Russia attacked Finland – *Pamir* idle at Goteburg

Depart Goteborg (in ballast) March 1940, arrive Bahia Blanca May 1940, 69 days
Depart Bahia Blanca (after layup), arrive Seychelles Islands
Depart Seychelles Islands (guano) October 1940, arrive New Plymouth Dec. 1940, 56 days
Depart New Plymouth (in ballast) February 1941, arrive Seychelles Islands
Depart Seychelles Islands (guano), arrive Wellington July 1941

August 1941 – vessel seized in prize – refit and preparation for New Zealand service

UNDER NEW ZEALAND FLAG

Depart Wellington (wool and tallow) March 1942, arrive San Francisco May 1942, 58 days
Depart San Francisco (bitumen and petroleum products) July 1942, arrive Wellington Sept. 1942, 68 days
Depart Wellington (wool and tallow) Nov. 1942, arrive San Francisco Jan. 1943, 78 days
Depart San Francisco (misc.) March 1943, arrive Wellington June 1943, 66 days
Depart Wellington (wool and tallow) July 1943, arrive San Francisco Oct. 1943, 80 days
Depart San Francisco (misc.) Dec. 1943, arrive Wellington Feb. 1944, 58 days
Depart Wellington (wool and tallow) March 1944, arrive San Francisco June 1944, 79 days
Depart San Francisco (misc.) July 1944, arrive Wellington Sept. 1944, 51 days
Depart Wellington (wool and tallow) Oct. 1944, arrive San Francisco Nov. 1944, 51 days
Depart San Francisco (misc.) Jan. 1945, arrive Wellington March 1945, 54 days
Depart Wellington (wool and tallow) April 1945, arrive Vancouver June 1945, 59 days
Depart Vancouver (wheat) July 1945, arrive Wellington Aug. 1945, 48 days
Depart Wellington (wool and tallow) Sept. 1945, arrive Vancouver Nov. 1945, 67 days
Depart Vancouver (wheat) Jan. 1946, arrive Wellington March 1946, 65 days
Depart Wellington (wool and tallow) May 1946, arrive Vancouver July 1946, 58 days
Vessel towed to Union Bay, Vancouver Island

Depart Union Bay (coal) Aug. 1946, arrive Wellington Oct. 1946, 56 days

Depart Wellington (in ballast) Nov. 1946, arrive Lyttleton Nov. 1946
Depart Lyttleton (timber) Dec. 1946, arrive Sydney Jan. 1947, 15 days
Depart Sydney (cement) April 1947, arrive Wellington April 1947, 12 days

Depart Wellington (wool) Oct. 1947, arrive Gravesend Dec. 1947, 80 days
Depart London (cement) April 1948, arrive Antwerp April 1948
Completed cargo – slag
Depart Antwerp May 1948, arrive Auckland August 1948, 107 days
Depart Auckland (in ballast) Sept. 1948, arrive Wellington October 1948

November 1948 – vessel formally restored to Finland – refit

UNDER FINNISH FLAG

Depart Wellington (in ballast) Feb. 1949, arrive Port Victoria March 1949, 34 days
Depart Port Victoria (grain) May 1949, arrive Falmouth Oct. 1949, 128 days
Discharge at Penarth

March 1951 – after being laid up as a store ship, vessel towed to Antwerp having been sold to ship breakers

UNDER GERMAN FLAG

June 1951 – vessel towed to Travemunde after being bought for use as cargo-carrying training ship

Sept. 1951 – vessel towed to Kiel for extensive alterations including installation of auxiliary engine

Depart Hamburg (cement) Jan. 1952, arrive Rio de Janeiro Feb. 1952, 49 days
Depart Vitoria (ore) April 1952, arrive Rotterdam May 1952

Depart Bremen (cement) 1952, arrive Santos 1952
Depart Buenos Aires (wheat) 1952, arrive Antwerp October 1952

October 1952 – at Rotterdam to load but owner in bankruptcy and vessel taken to Hamburg and laid up 1953

April 1954 – vessel sold by auction
1955 – vessel taken over by association of German ship owners at Lubeck
January 1955 – vessel drydocked and refit

Depart Hamburg (in ballast) 1955, arrive Buenos Aires 1955
Depart Buenos Aires (wheat) 1955, arrive Hamburg 1955

Depart Hamburg (cement) 1955, arrive Paranagua 1955
Depart Bahia Blanca (wheat) 1955, arrive Brake Nov. 1955

Vessel overhauled at Bremen

Depart Bremen (coke) 1956, arrive Montevideo-Buenos Aires 1956
Depart Rosario (wheat) 1956, arrive Hamburg 1956

1956 – vessel underwent extensive refit

Depart Hamburg (coke) 1956, arrive Buenos Aires 1956
Depart Buenos Aires (barley) 1956, arrive Hamburg 1956

Depart Antwerp (methyl alcohol) 1957, arrive Montevideo 1957
Depart Montevideo (barley) 1957, arrive Hamburg 1957

1957 May-June – vessel lying at yard of Blohm and Voss, Hamburg

Depart Hamburg (in ballast) June 1957, arrive Buenos Aires July 1957
Depart Buenos Aires (barley) Aug. 1957. Vessel lost en route Sept. 1957